Good Food Made Simple

PASTA

Over 140 delicious recipes, 500 color photographs, step-by-step images, and nutritional information

This edition published by Parragon Books Ltd in 2013 and distributed by

Parragon Inc.
440 Park Avenue South, 13th Floor
New York, NY 10016
www.parragon.com/lovefood

LOVE FOOD is an imprint of Parragon Books Ltd
Copyright © Parragon Books Ltd 2012–2013

LOVE FOOD and the accompanying heart device is a registered trademark of
Parragon Books Ltd in the USA, the UK, Australia, India, and the EU.

ISBN 978-1-4723-4677-3

Printed in China

Cover design by Lexi L'Esteve
Cover photography by Mike Cooper
New photography by Clive Bozzard-Hill
New home economy by Valerie Barrett, Carol Tennant, Sally Mansfield
and Mitzie Wilson
New recipes and introduction by Linda Doeser
Edited by Fiona Biggs
Nutritional analysis by Fiona Hunter

Notes for the Reader
This book uses standard kitchen measuring spoons and cups. All spoon and cup
measurements are level unless otherwise indicated. Unless otherwise stated,
milk is assumed to be whole, eggs are large, individual vegetables are medium,
and pepper is freshly ground black pepper. Unless otherwise stated, all root
vegetables should be peeled prior to using.

Garnishes, decorations, and serving suggestions are all optional and not
necessarily included in the recipe ingredients or method. Any optional
ingredients and seasoning to taste are not included in the nutritional analysis. The
times given are only an approximate guide. Preparation times differ according
to the techniques used by different people and the cooking times may also vary
from those given. Optional ingredients, variations, or serving suggestions have
not been included in the time calculations.

Spaghetti with Meat Sauce *18*

Meatballs in a Creamy Sauce *20*

Rare Beef Pasta Salad *22*

Ground Beef & Pasta Soup *24*

Pasta with Beef Rolls *26*

Sausage, Bean & Roasted Squash Conchiglie *28*

Tagliatelle with a Rich Meat Sauce *30*

Beef Stroganoff *32*

Hamburger Pasta *34*

Spaghetti & Corned Beef *36*

Spaghetti with Meatloaf *38*

Beef Macaroni *40*

Spaghetti Carbonara *42*

Spaghetti with Bacon & Crispy Bread Crumbs *44*

Pasta with Bacon & Tomatoes *46*

Creamy Pasta with Bacon *48*

Spicy Pasta Amatriciana *50*

Saffron Linguine *52*

Penne Pasta with Sausage *54*

Spicy Sausage Salad *56*

Italian Sausage & Pasta Soup *58*

Pepperoni Pasta *60*

Rigatoni with Chorizo & Mushrooms *62*

Linguine With Lamb & Yellow Pepper Sauce *64*

Meat

Spaghetti with Meat Sauce

 SERVES 4 — PREP TIME: 15 minutes — COOKING TIME: 1 hour

nutritional information per serving	535 cal, 14g fat, 4g sat fat, 5g total sugars, 0.4g salt

This classic meat sauce (ragù) from Bologna can also be made with ground veal or half beef and half pork.

INGREDIENTS

12 ounces spaghetti or pasta of your choice

fresh Parmesan cheese shavings, to garnish (optional)

sprigs of thyme, to garnish

crusty bread, to serve

meat sauce

2 tablespoons olive oil

1 onion, finely chopped

2 garlic cloves, finely chopped

1 carrot, peeled and finely chopped

1 cup quartered white button mushrooms (optional)

1 teaspoon dried oregano

½ teaspoon dried thyme

1 bay leaf

10 ounces lean ground beef

1¼ cups stock

1¼ cups tomato puree

pepper

1. To make the sauce, heat the oil in a heavy, nonstick saucepan. Add the onion and sauté, half covered, for 5 minutes, or until soft. Add the garlic, carrot, and mushrooms, if using, and sauté for an additional 3 minutes, stirring occasionally.

2. Add the herbs and ground beef to the pan and cook until the meat has browned, stirring regularly.

3. Add the stock and tomato puree. Reduce the heat, season with pepper, and cook over medium–low heat, half covered, for 15–20 minutes, or until the sauce has reduced and thickened. Remove and discard the bay leaf.

4. Meanwhile, bring a large saucepan of lightly salted water to a boil. Add the pasta, bring back to a boil, and cook for 8–10 minutes, or according to the package directions, until tender but still firm to the bite. Drain well and mix together the pasta and sauce until the pasta is well coated. Garnish with the Parmesan cheese, if using, and sprigs of thyme. Serve immediately, with the crusty bread.

Meatballs in a Creamy Sauce

 SERVES 6

PREP TIME: 35 minutes

COOKING TIME: 15 minutes

nutritional information per serving	690 cal, 30g fat, 13g sat fat, 5g total sugars, 0.6g salt

This delicious regional speciality comes from Minnesota in the Midwest, with its twin cities of Minneapolis and St. Paul.

INGREDIENTS

1 cup fresh bread crumbs

¾ cup whole milk

1 small onion, chopped

1 garlic clove, chopped

12 ounces fresh ground beef

8 ounces fresh ground pork

4 ounces fresh ground veal

¼ cup mashed potato

⅔ cup freshly grated Parmesan cheese

½ teaspoon ground allspice

1 tablespoon chopped fresh flat-leaf parsley, plus extra to garnish

1 tablespoon chopped sage

1 egg

⅓ cup all-purpose flour

1 pound dried spaghetti

2 tablespoons olive oil

¾ cup light cream

salt and pepper

1. Put the bread crumbs into a small bowl, add the milk, and let soak. Put the onion and garlic into a food processor and process to a puree. Scrape into a large bowl and add the beef, pork, veal, potato, cheese, allspice, parsley, sage, and egg. Drain the bread crumbs and add to the bowl. Season with salt and pepper and mix well.

2. Shape the mixture into balls about 1 inch in diameter by rolling the mixture between the palms of your hands. Put ¼ cup of the flour in a shallow dish and roll the meatballs in it to coat.

3. Bring a large saucepan of lightly salted water to a boil. Add the pasta, bring back to a boil, and cook for 8–10 minutes, or according to the package directions, until tender but still firm to the bite.

4. Meanwhile, heat the oil in a skillet, add the meatballs, and cook over medium heat, shaking the skillet occasionally, for 10 minutes, until evenly browned and cooked all the way through. Remove with a slotted spoon and keep warm.

5. Stir the remaining flour into the cooking juices in the skillet. Add the cream and mix for 3–4 minutes, but do not let the mixture boil. Season with salt and pepper and remove from the heat.

6. Drain the pasta and divide among six plates, then top with the meatballs. Spoon the sauce over the pasta and serve immediately.

Rare Beef Pasta Salad

 SERVES 4 PREP TIME: 15 minutes 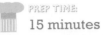 COOKING TIME: 25–30 minutes

nutritional information per serving	671 cal, 18g fat, 4g sat fat, 10g total sugars, 1.6g salt

Thai fish sauce, also known as nam pla, is made from salted anchovies and has a strong flavor, so use it with discretion. It is available from some supermarkets and from Asian grocery stores.

INGREDIENTS

1 pound top sirloin steak or tenderloin steak (in 1 piece)

1 pound dried fusilli

¼ cup olive oil

2 tablespoons lime juice

2 tablespoons Thai fish sauce

2 teaspoon honey

4 scallions, sliced

1 cucumber, peeled and cut into 1-inch chunks

3 tomatoes, cut into wedges

3 teaspoons finely chopped fresh mint

salt and pepper

1. Season the steak with salt and pepper, then broil or pan-fry for 4 minutes on each side. Let rest for 5 minutes, then, using a sharp knife, slice the steak thinly across the grain and reserve until required.

2. Meanwhile, bring a large saucepan of lightly salted water to a boil. Add the pasta, bring back to a boil, and cook for 8–10 minutes, or according to the package directions, until tender but still firm to the bite. Drain thoroughly and toss in the oil.

3. Mix together the lime juice, fish sauce, and honey in a small saucepan and cook over medium heat for about 2 minutes.

4. Add the scallions, cucumber, tomato wedges, and mint to the pan, then add the steak and mix well. Season with salt.

5. Transfer the pasta to a large, warm serving dish and top with the steak mixture. Serve just warm or let cool completely.

Hamburger Pasta

 SERVES 4

PREP TIME:
10 minutes

COOKING TIME:
15 minutes

nutritional information per serving	686 cal, 34g fat, 12g sat fat, 8g total sugars, 0.9g salt

This is a good way to use up extra hamburger patties, combining them with staple ingredients for a quick meal.

INGREDIENTS

10 ounces dried conchiglie (pasta shells)

12 ounces hamburger patties

1 (16-ounce) package frozen mixed vegetables, such as carrots, corn, and broccoli or green beans

1 (14½-ounce) can tomatoes, drained

1 garlic clove, finely chopped

1–1½ pickled jalapeño chiles, finely chopped

3 tablespoons olive oil

2 tablespoons freshly grated Parmesan cheese

salt and pepper

1. Preheat the broiler. Bring a large saucepan of lightly salted water to a boil. Add the pasta, bring back to a boil, and cook for 8–10 minutes, or according to the package directions, until tender but still firm to the bite.

2. Cook the hamburger patties under the preheated broiler for 7–8 minutes on each side until cooked through. Meanwhile, bring a separate saucepan of lightly salted water to a boil, add the frozen vegetables, and cook for about 5 minutes.

3. Drain the vegetables, transfer to a food processor, and process briefly until chopped, then put into a saucepan. Transfer the cooked burgers to the food processor and process briefly until chopped, then add to the pan of vegetables. Stir in the tomatoes, garlic, chiles, and oil, season with salt and pepper, and reheat gently.

4. Drain the pasta and put it into a warm serving bowl. Add the burger-and-vegetable mixture and toss lightly. Sprinkle with the cheese and serve immediately.

SOMETHING DIFFERENT

If serving to young children or if you just don't like spicy food, omit the chiles and add a pinch of dried oregano instead.

Spaghetti & Corned Beef

 SERVES 4

PREP TIME: 15 minutes

COOKING TIME: 25–30 minutes

nutritional information per serving	742 cal, 21g fat, 8g sat fat, 8g total sugars, 2.8g salt

This variation of corned beef and hash will be popular with children and is also economical, and it is an easy way to make a change in the normal family menu.

INGREDIENTS

2 tablespoons sunflower oil

1 large onion, chopped

2–3 garlic cloves, finely chopped

1 pound corned beef, chopped

1 (14½-ounce) canned tomatoes

1 pound dried spaghetti

2 tablespoons chopped fresh parsley

pinch of crushed red pepper or dash of Tabasco sauce or Worcestershire sauce

salt and pepper

1. Heat the oil in a large skillet, add the onion and garlic, and cook over medium heat for 5 minutes, until just beginning to brown.

2. Add the corned beef and cook, stirring and mashing with a wooden spoon, for 5–8 minutes, until it is dry. Drain the tomatoes, reserving the can juices, and stir them into the skillet. Cook for an additional 10 minutes, adding a little of the reserved can juices if the mixture seems to be drying out too much.

3. Meanwhile, bring a large saucepan of lightly salted water to a boil. Add the pasta, bring back to a boil, and cook for 8–10 minutes, or according to the package directions, until tender but still firm to the bite.

4. Drain the pasta and add it to the skillet. Stir in the parsley and crushed red pepper and season with salt and pepper, keeping in mind that corned beef is often already salty. Mix well and heat through for an additional few minutes. Serve immediately.

HEALTHY HINT
You can buy cans of reduced-salt corned beef if you are concerned about the levels of salt in your diet.

Beef Macaroni

SERVES 4–6

PREP TIME: 15 minutes

COOKING TIME: 1 hour

nutritional information per serving	355 cal, 17g fat, 7.5g sat fat, 7g total sugars, 0.8g salt

This is a terrific dish for easy entertaining, especially because you can have it ready to go in the oven before your guests arrive.

INGREDIENTS

2 tablespoons olive oil

1 onion, chopped

2 garlic cloves, finely chopped

1 pound top sirloin steak, cut into thin strips

2 tablespoons tomato paste

1 tablespoon all-purpose flour

1 tablespoon sweet paprika

1¼ cups hot beef stock

4 ounces dried elbow macaroni

2 beefsteak tomatoes, sliced

2 cups Greek-style yogurt

2 eggs, lightly beaten

salt and pepper

1. Heat the oil in a large saucepan, add the onion and garlic, and cook over low heat, stirring occasionally, for 5 minutes. Add the steak, increase the heat to medium, and cook, stirring frequently, for 2–3 minutes, or until evenly browned.

2. Stir in the tomato paste, sprinkle in the flour and paprika, and cook, stirring, for 1 minute. Stir in the stock, season with salt and pepper, and bring to a boil. Reduce the heat and simmer for 10 minutes.

3. Meanwhile, preheat the oven to 375°F. Bring a saucepan of lightly salted water to a boil. Add the pasta, bring back to a boil, and cook for 8–10 minutes, or according to the package directions, until tender but still firm to the bite.

4. Spoon the steak mixture into an ovenproof dish and cover with the tomato slices. Drain the pasta, put it into a bowl, and stir in the yogurt and eggs. Spoon the pasta on top of the tomatoes and bake in the preheated oven for 30 minutes. Remove from the oven and serve immediately.

GOES WELL WITH
This substantial
dish requires
nothing more than
a mixed green
salad with some
herbs and a light
dressing.

Spaghetti Carbonara

SERVES 4   PREP TIME: 15 minutes   COOKING TIME: 25–30 minutes

nutritional information per serving	1,498 cal, 73g fat, 35g sat fat, 7g total sugars, 4g salt

This popular Italian dish combines pancetta and heavy cream with 2 hard cheeses—Parmesan and pecorino.

INGREDIENTS

1 pound dried spaghetti

4 eggs

¼ cup heavy cream

⅔ cup grated Parmesan cheese, plus extra to garnish

⅔ cup grated pecorino cheese

1 tablespoon butter

6 ounces pancetta, finely diced

salt and pepper

1. Bring a large saucepan of lightly salted water to a boil. Add the pasta, bring back to a boil, and cook for 8–10 minutes, or according to the package directions, until tender but still firm to the bite.

2. Meanwhile, stir together the eggs, cream, Parmesan cheese, and pecorino cheese in a bowl. Season with salt and pepper.

3. Melt the butter in a large saucepan, add the pancetta, and cook over medium heat for 8-10 minutes, until crispy. Drain the spaghetti and add it to the pan while still dripping wet. Pour the cheese sauce over spaghetti. Remove the pan from the heat. Toss the spaghetti in the sauce until the eggs begin to thicken but are still creamy.

4. Transfer to warm plates and serve immediately, sprinkled with pepper and a little more Parmesan cheese.

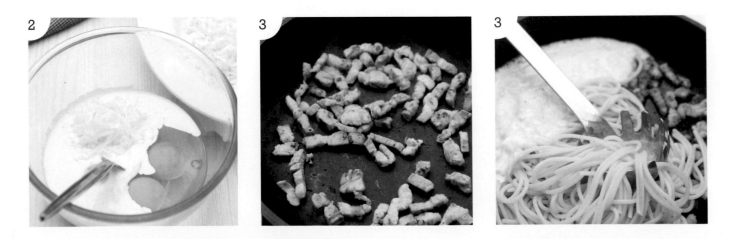

COOKS NOTE

For a more substantial dish, cook 1-2 finely chopped shallots with the pancetta and add 2 cups sliced button mushrooms.

Spaghetti with Bacon & Crispy Bread Crumbs

SERVES 2   PREP TIME: 10 minutes   COOKING TIME: 20 minutes

nutritional information per serving	787 cal, 42g fat, 11g sat fat, 4g total sugars, 2.7g salt

Quick, easy, and economical, yet truly mouthwatering, this is the perfect midweek family dinner.

INGREDIENTS

1 day-old ciabatta roll
sprig of fresh rosemary
6 ounces dried spaghetti
2 teaspoons olive oil
5 ounces smoked bacon, chopped
1 tablespoon butter
⅓ cup pine nuts
2 garlic cloves, crushed
2–3 tablespoons chopped fresh flat-leaf parsley
salt and pepper

1. Put the day-old bread, including any crusts, in a food processor or blender and process until the mixture resembles coarse bread crumbs. Bruise the rosemary sprig in a mortar and pestle or using a rolling pin to release the flavor.

2. Bring a large saucepan of lightly salted water to a boil. Add the pasta, bring back to a boil, and cook for 8–10 minutes, or according to the package directions, until tender but still firm to the bite.

3. Meanwhile, heat the oil in a large skillet, add the bacon and rosemary, and sauté for 2–3 minutes, until the bacon is golden brown. Transfer to a warm serving bowl using a slotted spoon.

4. Add the butter to the bacon fat remaining in the skillet. When melted and foaming, add the bread crumbs, pine nuts, and garlic. Sauté for 2–3 minutes, stirring until golden brown, then put into the bowl with the bacon.

5. Drain the pasta and transfer to the bowl with the bacon and bread crumbs. Add the parsley, season with pepper, and toss well. Serve immediately.

Pasta with Bacon & Tomatoes

 SERVES 4

PREP TIME:
10 minutes

COOKING TIME:
35–40 minutes

nutritional information per serving	592 cal, 17g fat, 8g sat fat, 10g total sugars, 1.5g salt

This is an ideal dish to serve in the summer, when tomatoes are at their sweetest.

INGREDIENTS

10 small, sweet tomatoes (about 2 pounds)

6 rindless smoked bacon strips

4 tablespoons butter

1 onion, chopped

1 garlic clove, crushed

4 fresh oregano sprigs, finely chopped

1 pound dried orecchiette ("little ears") pasta

salt and pepper

freshly grated pecorino cheese, to serve

1. Blanch the tomatoes in boiling water. Drain, peel, and seed the tomatoes, then coarsely chop the flesh.

2. Using a sharp knife, chop the bacon into small dice. Melt the butter in a saucepan. Add the bacon and cook for 2-3 minutes, until golden brown.

3. Add the onion and garlic and cook over medium heat for 5–7 minutes, until just softened. Add the tomatoes and oregano to the pan, then season with salt and pepper. Lower the heat and simmer for 10–12 minutes.

4. Meanwhile, bring a large saucepan of lightly salted water to a boil. Add the pasta, bring back to a boil, and cook for 8–10 minutes, or according to the package directions, until tender but still firm to the bite. Drain the pasta and transfer to a warm serving bowl. Spoon the bacon-and-tomato sauce over the pasta, toss to coat, and serve immediately with the pecorino cheese.

1

3

4

Creamy Pasta with Bacon

SERVES 6

PREP TIME:
10 minutes

COOKING TIME:
15 minutes

nutritional information per serving	510 cal, 21g fat, 12g sat fat, 6g total sugars, 1g salt

This is an updated version of a Hungarian dish called turos csusza, originally consisting of noodles, sheep cheese, bacon, and smetana (a type of sour cream).

INGREDIENTS

1 pound dried pasta spirals or elbow macaroni
4 smoked bacon strips
2 cups sour cream
1½ cups cottage cheese
salt

1. Preheat the oven to 350°F and preheat the broiler. Bring a large saucepan of lightly salted water to a boil, add the pasta, bring back to a boil, and cook for 8–10 minutes, or according to the package directions, until tender but still firm to the bite.

2. Meanwhile, cook the bacon under the preheated broiler for 3–4 minutes on each side, until crisp. Remove from the heat and crumble.

3. Drain the pasta, put it into an ovenproof dish, and stir in the sour cream. Sprinkle with the cottage cheese, then with the crumbled bacon, and lightly season with salt. Bake in the preheated oven for 5 minutes, then serve straight from the dish.

2   3   3

SOMETHING DIFFERENT

For a stronger, more authentic flavor, substitute crumbled feta cheese for the cottage cheese.

Spicy Pasta Amatriciana

 SERVES 4   PREP TIME: 25 minutes   COOKING TIME: 30 minutes

nutritional information per serving	694 cal, 24g fat, 9g sat fat, 11g total sugars, 2g salt

Traditionally served with bucatini, this dish from the town of Amatrice in central Italy is served to celebrate the national August holiday.

INGREDIENTS

2 tablespoons olive oil

1 large onion, finely chopped

2 garlic cloves, finely chopped

6 ounces pancetta or bacon, diced

1–2 red chiles, seeded and chopped, or ½–1 teaspoon crushed red pepper

3 tablespoons dry white wine

1 (28-ounce) can diced tomatoes

1 pound dried bucatini or spaghetti

1 cup freshly grated pecorino cheese

salt and pepper

1. Heat the oil in a large saucepan, add the onion and garlic, and cook over low heat, stirring occasionally, for 5 minutes. Add the pancetta and chiles, increase the heat to medium, and cook, stirring frequently, for 5–8 minutes, until the onion is lightly browned.

2. Pour in the wine, bring to a boil, and boil rapidly for 2 minutes, then stir in the tomatoes and season with salt and pepper. Bring back to a boil, then reduce the heat to low and simmer, stirring occasionally, for 15 minutes.

3. Meanwhile, bring a large saucepan of lightly salted water to a boil. Add the pasta, bring back to a boil, and cook for 8–10 minutes, or according to the package directions, until tender but still firm to the bite.

4. Drain the pasta, put into the pan with the sauce, and toss to coat. Transfer to a warm serving dish, sprinkle with half the cheese, and serve immediately, with the remaining cheese on the side.

SOMETHING DIFFERENT

For additional flavor, add 1 tablespoon of chopped flat-leaf parsley, 5-6 torn basil leaves, or a generous pinch of dried oregano to the tomatoes.

Saffron Linguine

SERVES 4

PREP TIME:
10 minutes

COOKING TIME:
25–30 minutes

nutritional information per serving	650 cal, 33g fat, 19g sat fat, 3g total sugars, 1.3g salt

Saffron gives this delightful dish its delicate color, pungently sweet aroma, and unique flavor.

INGREDIENTS

12 ounces dried linguine

pinch of saffron threads

2 tablespoons water

5 ounces cooked ham, cut into strips

¾ cup heavy cream

⅔ cup freshly grated Parmesan cheese

2 egg yolks

salt and pepper

1. Bring a large saucepan of lightly salted water to a boil. Add the pasta, bring back to a boil, and cook for 8–10 minutes, or according to the package directions, until tender but still firm to the bite.

2. Meanwhile, place the saffron in a saucepan and add the water. Bring to a boil, then remove from the heat and let stand for 5 minutes.

3. Stir the ham, cream, and cheese into the saffron and return the pan to the heat. Season with salt and pepper and heat through gently, stirring continuously, until simmering. Remove from the heat and beat in the egg yolks. Drain the pasta and transfer to a warm serving dish. Add the saffron sauce, toss well, and serve immediately.

2

3

3
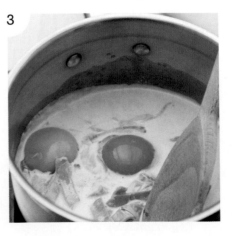

VARIATION
You don't have to use cooked ham in this dish. For a richer flavor, try using prosciutto, or even bacon.

Penne Pasta with Sausage

SERVES 4–6 **PREP TIME:** 15 minutes **COOKING TIME:** 30–35 minutes

nutritional information per serving	437 cal, 19g fat, 6g sat fat, 5g total sugars, 1.5g salt

Packed with flavor and lively rather than fiery, this is an ideal dish for informal entertaining.

INGREDIENTS

2 tablespoons olive oil

1 red onion, coarsely chopped

2 garlic cloves, coarsely chopped

6 Italian link sausages, skinned and the meat crumbled

½ teaspoon crushed red pepper

2 tablespoons chopped fresh oregano

1 (14½-ounce) can diced tomatoes

12 ounces dried penne

salt and pepper

1. Heat the oil in a large saucepan, add the onion, and cook over medium heat, stirring frequently, for 6–8 minutes, until starting to brown. Add the garlic and the crumbled sausages and cook for 8–10 minutes, breaking up the sausages with a wooden spoon.

2. Add the crushed red pepper and oregano and stir well. Pour in the tomatoes and bring to a boil. Place over low heat and simmer for 4–5 minutes, until reduced and thickened. Season with salt and pepper.

3. Meanwhile, bring a large saucepan of lightly salted water to a boil. Add the pasta, bring back to a boil, and cook for 8–10 minutes, or according to the package directions, until tender but still firm to the bite. Drain thoroughly and return to the pan.

4. Pour the sauce into the pasta and stir well. Transfer to warm serving plates and serve immediately.

1

2

3
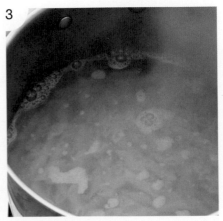

COOKS NOTE

Italian link-style sausages are popular for their spicy flavor. However, if you can't find them, use any good-quality pork link sausages instead.

Italian Sausage & Pasta Soup

 SERVES 4   PREP TIME: 20 minutes   COOKING TIME: 45 minutes

nutritional information per serving	552 cal, 27g fat, 9g sat fat, 9g total sugars, 3.5g salt

Served with some crusty bread, this filling soup makes a meal in a bowl—ideal for family lunch on busy weekends.

INGREDIENTS

2 tablespoons olive oil

1 onion, chopped

1 carrot, chopped

1 celery stalk, chopped

1 pound Italian link sausages, skinned and crumbled

2 garlic cloves, finely chopped

2 bay leaves

½ teaspoon dried oregano

1 teaspoon crushed red pepper (optional)

1 (14½-ounce) can diced tomatoes

3½ cups chicken stock

1 (15-ounce) can cannellini beans, drained

4 ounces dried soup pasta shapes

2 tablespoons chopped fresh flat-leaf parsley

salt and pepper

freshly grated Parmesan cheese, to serve

1. Heat the oil in a large saucepan, add the onion, carrot, and celery, and cook over low heat, stirring occasionally, for 5 minutes. Stir in the crumbled sausages and garlic, increase the heat to medium, and cook, stirring frequently, for an additional few minutes, until the meat is brown.

2. Add the bay leaves, oregano, crushed red pepper, if using, tomatoes, and stock, and bring to a boil, stirring frequently. Reduce the heat, partly cover, and simmer for 30 minutes.

3. Stir in the beans and pasta and simmer for another 5–8 minutes, until the pasta is tender but still firm to the bite. Season with salt and pepper, stir in the parsley, and remove from the heat. Remove and discard the bay leaves, ladle the soup into warm mugs or bowls, and serve immediately, with the cheese separately.

Pepperoni Pasta

 SERVES 4   PREP TIME: 10 minutes   COOKING TIME: 20 minutes

nutritional information **per serving**   780 cal, 33g fat, 10g sat fat, 14g total sugars, 2.8g salt

A sure-fire favorite, this colorful and delicious dish will brighten up even a truly dull day.

INGREDIENTS

3 tablespoons olive oil
1 onion, chopped
1 red bell pepper, seeded and diced
1 orange bell pepper, seeded and diced
1 (28-ounce) can diced tomatoes
1 tablespoon tomato paste
1 teaspoon paprika
8 ounces pepperoni sausage, sliced
2 tablespoons chopped flat-leaf parsley, plus extra to garnish
1 pound dried penne
salt and pepper

1. Heat 2 tablespoons of the oil in a large, heavy skillet. Add the onion and cook over low heat, stirring occasionally, for 5 minutes, or until softened. Add the red bell pepper, orange bell pepper, tomatoes and their can juices, tomato paste, and paprika and bring to a boil.

2. Add the pepperoni and parsley and season with salt and pepper. Stir well, bring to a boil, then reduce the heat and simmer for 10–15 minutes.

3. Meanwhile, bring a large saucepan of lightly salted water to a boil. Add the pasta, bring back to a boil, and cook for 8–10 minutes, or according to the package directions, until tender but still firm to the bite. Drain well and transfer to a warm serving dish. Add the remaining olive oil and toss. Add the sauce and toss again. Sprinkle with parsley and serve immediately.

COOKS NOTE

Pepperoni is a hot, spicy Italian sausage made from pork and beef and flavored with fennel. You could substitute another spicy sausage, such as chorizo.

Rigatoni with Chorizo & Mushrooms

SERVES 4

PREP TIME:
15 minutes

COOKING TIME:
25–30 minutes

nutritional information per serving	668 cal, 29g fat, 9g sat fat, 6g total sugars, 1g salt

This is a delightfully rustic and earthy dish—real comfort food that is also quick and easy to prepare.

INGREDIENTS

¼ cup olive oil

1 red onion, chopped

1 garlic clove, chopped

1 celery stalk, sliced

1 pound dried rigatoni

10 ounces chorizo sausage, sliced

8 ounces cremini mushrooms, halved

1 tablespoon chopped fresh cilantro

1 tablespoon lime juice

salt and pepper

1. Heat the oil in a skillet. Add the onion, garlic, and celery and cook over low heat, stirring occasionally, for 5 minutes, until softened.

2. Meanwhile, bring a large saucepan of lightly salted water to a boil. Add the pasta, bring back to a boil, and cook for 8–10 minutes, or according to the package directions, until tender but still firm to the bite.

3. While the pasta is cooking, add the chorizo to the skillet and cook, stirring occasionally, for 5 minutes, until evenly browned. Add the mushrooms and cook, stirring occasionally, for an additional 5 minutes. Stir in the cilantro and lime juice, and season with salt and pepper.

4. Drain the pasta and return it to the pan. Add the chorizo-and-mushroom mixture and toss. Divide among warm plates and serve immediately.

GOES WELL WITH
Cheese focaccia, warm
ciabatta with sun-dried
tomatoes, or plain hot
rolls will turn this
dish into a feast.

Linguine with Lamb & Yellow Pepper Sauce

SERVES 4

PREP TIME: 15 minutes

COOKING TIME: 1¼ hours

nutritional information per serving	485 cal, 18g fat, 4.5g sat fat, 9g total sugars, 0.2g salt

This unusual and richly flavored dish is a speciality from Sicily, an island where pasta features in at least one meal every day.

INGREDIENTS

¼ cup olive oil

10 ounces boneless lamb cutlets, cubed

1 garlic clove, finely chopped

1 bay leaf

½ cup dry white wine

2 large yellow bell peppers, seeded and diced

4 tomatoes, peeled and chopped

8 ounces dried linguine

salt and pepper

1. Heat half the olive oil in a large, heavy skillet. Add the lamb and cook over medium heat, stirring frequently, until browned on all sides. Add the garlic and cook for an additional minute. Add the bay leaf, pour in the wine, and season with salt and pepper. Bring to a boil and cook for 5 minutes, or until reduced.

2. Stir in the remaining oil, bell peppers, and tomatoes. Reduce the heat, cover, and simmer, stirring occasionally, for 45 minutes.

3. Meanwhile, bring a large saucepan of lightly salted water to a boil. Add the pasta, bring back to a boil, and cook for 8–10 minutes, until tender but still firm to the bite. Drain and transfer to a warm serving dish. Remove and discard the bay leaf from the lamb sauce, spoon the sauce over the pasta, and toss. Serve immediately.

1

2

2

GOES WELL WITH
A simple mixed green salad with a lemon vinaigrette dressing would be a refreshing accompaniment for this hearty dish.

Farfalle with Chicken & Broccoli *68*

Fettuccine with Chicken & Onion Cream Sauce *70*

Italian Chicken Soup *72*

Chicken Soup with Angel-Hair Pasta *74*

Chicken, Bacon & Avocado Salad *76*

Honey & Chicken Pasta Salad *78*

Pasta, Chicken & Grape Salad *80*

Pappardelle with Chicken & Porcini Mushrooms *82*

Chicken Meatball Pasta *84*

Chicken with Creamy Penne *86*

Spaghetti with Parsley Chicken *88*

Cajun Chicken Pasta *90*

Penne with Chicken & Feta Cheese *92*

Pasta with Chicken & Bell Peppers *94*

Pasta with Two Sauces *96*

Turkey & Pasta Soup *98*

Mexican Spaghetti & Meatballs *100*

Turkey Tetrazzini *102*

Jumbo Pasta Shells with Turkey *104*

Turkey Pasta Primavera *106*

Pasta with Chili Barbecue Sauce *108*

Pasta with Harissa Turkey Meatballs *110*

Fettuccine with Duck Sauce *112*

Venetian Duck with Spaghetti *114*

Poultry

Fettuccine with Chicken & Onion Cream Sauce

 SERVES 4

PREP TIME:
10 minutes

COOKING TIME:
35 minutes

nutritional information per serving	1,087 cal, 57g fat, 32g sat fat, 8g total sugars, 1.4g salt

The impressively luxurious taste belies the simplicity of this dish and the ease with which it can be prepared.

INGREDIENTS

1 tablespoon olive oil

2 tablespoons butter

1 garlic clove, minced

4 skinless, boneless chicken breasts

1 onion, finely chopped

1 chicken bouillon cube, crumbled

½ cup water

1¼ cups heavy cream

¾ cup whole milk

6 scallions, green part included, sliced diagonally

½ cup freshly grated Parmesan cheese

1 pound dried fettuccine

salt and pepper

chopped fresh flat-leaf parsley, to garnish

1. Heat the oil and butter with the garlic in a large skillet over medium–low heat. Cook the garlic until just beginning to brown. Add the chicken and increase the heat to medium. Cook for 4–5 minutes on each side, until cooked through and the juices run clear. Season with salt and pepper. Remove from the heat. Remove the chicken from the skillet, leaving the oil in the skillet. Slice the chicken diagonally into thin strips and set aside.

2. Reheat the oil in the skillet. Add the onion and gently cook for 5 minutes, until soft. Add the crumbled bouillon cube and the water. Bring to a boil, then simmer over medium–low heat for 10 minutes. Stir in the cream, milk, scallions, and Parmesan cheese. Simmer until heated through and slightly thickened.

3. Meanwhile, bring a large saucepan of lightly salted water to a boil. Add the pasta, bring back to a boil, and cook for 8–10 minutes, or according to the package directions, until tender but still firm to the bite. Drain and transfer to a warm serving dish. Layer the chicken slices over the pasta. Pour the sauce over the chicken and pasta, garnish with parsley, and serve immediately.

Chicken Soup with Angel-Hair Pasta

SERVES 6

PREP TIME:
10 minutes

COOKING TIME:
40 minutes

nutritional information per serving	252 cal, 10g fat, 2g sat fat, 0.5g total sugars, 0.9g salt

This is a truly filling and nourishing soup with a delicate flavor—the perfect lunchtime pick-me-up on a dull day.

INGREDIENTS

3 extra-large eggs

3 tablespoons water

2 tablespoons chopped fresh flat-leaf parsley

1 skinless, boneless chicken breast, about 6 ounces

2 tablespoons olive oil, plus extra for brushing

6½ cups chicken stock

4 ounces dried angel-hair pasta

salt and pepper

1. Preheat the broiler. Lightly beat the eggs with the water and a pinch of salt in a bowl and stir in the parsley. Season the chicken with salt and pepper and brush with oil. Broil for 4–5 minutes on each side, until cooked through and the juices run clear, then remove from the heat and cut into thin strips.

2. Heat the oil in an 8-inch omelet pan, then add one-quarter of the egg mixture, swirling the pan to spread it evenly. Cook over medium–low heat until the underside is set, then flip over with a spatula and cook for an additional few seconds. Slide the omelet out of the pan and reserve. Cook three more omelets in the same way, then roll them up and cut into thin slices to make threads.

3. Pour the stock into a large saucepan and bring to a boil. Add the pasta, bring back to a boil, and cook for 5 minutes, or according to the package directions, until tender but still firm to the bite. Add the chicken, season with salt and pepper, and cook for an additional 3–5 minutes. Stir in the omelet, remove from the heat, and serve immediately.

1

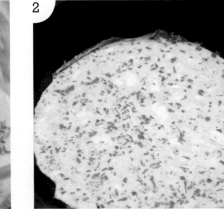

2

2

SOMETHING
DIFFERENT

This recipe also
works well with
cooked peeled shrimp
instead of broiled
chicken, replacing the
parsley with chopped
cilantro.

Honey & Chicken Pasta Salad

 SERVES 4   PREP TIME: 15 minutes   COOKING TIME: 25–30 minutes

nutritional information per serving	430 cal, 9g fat, 1.5g sat fat, 12g total sugars, 0.5g salt

This delectable salad with its wonderful combination of flavors is the perfect choice for an alfresco dinner on a warm summer's evening.

INGREDIENTS

8 ounces dried fusilli

2 tablespoons olive oil

1 onion, thinly sliced

1 garlic clove, crushed

2 skinless, boneless chicken breasts (about 14 ounces), thinly sliced

2 tablespoons whole-grain mustard

2 tablespoons honey

10 cherry tomatoes, halved

handful of arugula or mizuna leaves

fresh thyme leaves, to garnish

salt

dressing

3 tablespoons olive oil

1 tablespoon sherry vinegar

2 teaspoons honey

1 tablespoon fresh thyme leaves

salt and pepper

1. To make the dressing, place all the ingredients in a small bowl and beat together.

2. Bring a large saucepan of lightly salted water to a boil. Add the pasta, bring back to a boil, and cook for 8–10 minutes, or according to the package directions, until tender but still firm to the bite.

3. Meanwhile, heat the oil in a large skillet. Add the onion and garlic and sauté for 5 minutes.

4. Add the chicken and cook, stirring frequently, for 3–4 minutes, until cooked through. Stir the mustard and honey into the skillet and cook for an additional 2–3 minutes, until the chicken and onion are golden brown and sticky.

5. Drain the pasta and transfer to a serving bowl. Pour the dressing over the pasta and toss. Stir in the chicken and onion and let cool.

6. Gently stir the tomatoes and arugula into the pasta. Serve immediately garnished with the thyme leaves.

Pasta, Chicken & Grape Salad

 SERVES 2   PREP TIME: 15 minutes   COOKING TIME: 10–15 minutes

nutritional information per serving	707 cal, 36g fat, 6g sat fat, 16g total sugars, 0.4g salt

This is a delightfully elegant and truly delicious way to use up leftover cooked chicken.

INGREDIENTS

4–5 ounces dried fusilli

2 tablespoons mayonnaise

2 teaspoons pesto

1 tablespoon sour cream

1¼ cups cooked skinless, boneless chicken strips

1–2 celery stalks, sliced diagonally

1 cup halved seedless black grapes

1 large carrot, cut into strips

salt and pepper

celery leaves, to garnish

dressing

1 tablespoon white wine vinegar

3 tablespoons extra virgin olive oil

salt and pepper

1. To make the dressing, beat together the vinegar and oil, then season with salt and pepper.

2. Bring a large saucepan of lightly salted water to a boil. Add the pasta, bring back to a boil, and cook for 8–10 minutes, or according to the package directions, until tender but still firm to the bite. Drain thoroughly. Transfer to a bowl and mix in 1 tablespoon of the dressing while hot, then set aside until cold.

3. Combine the mayonnaise, pesto, and sour cream in a bowl, then season with salt and pepper.

4. Add the chicken, celery, grapes, carrot, and the mayonnaise mixture to the pasta and toss thoroughly. Check the seasoning, adding more salt and pepper, if necessary.

5. Arrange the pasta mixture in a large serving bowl, garnish with the celery leaves, and serve immediately with the reserved dressing.

1

3

4

GOES WELL WITH

A simple tomato and red onion salad with a basil-flavored vinaigrette is the perfect complement for this dish.

Pappardelle with Chicken & Porcini Mushrooms

SERVES 4   PREP TIME: 40 minutes   COOKING TIME: 1¼ hours

nutritional information per serving	519 cal, 12g fat, 2g sat fat, 7.5g total sugars, 0.3g salt

Wild mushrooms are used extensively in Italian dishes and porcini mushrooms are the most popular. When using porcini, always soak them first in hot water for 30 minutes, then drain well before cooking.

INGREDIENTS

1½ ounces dried porcini mushrooms

¾ cup hot water

1 (28-ounce) can diced tomatoes

1 fresh red chile, seeded and finely chopped

3 tablespoons olive oil

12 ounces skinless, boneless chicken, cut into thin strips

2 garlic cloves, finely chopped

12 ounces dried pappardelle

salt and pepper

2 tablespoons chopped fresh flat-leaf parsley, to garnish

1. Place the porcini in a small bowl, add the hot water, and soak for 30 minutes. Meanwhile, place the tomatoes and their can juices in a heavy saucepan and break them up with a wooden spoon, then stir in the chile. Bring to a boil, then reduce the heat and simmer, stirring occasionally, for 30 minutes, or until reduced.

2. Remove the mushrooms from their soaking liquid with a slotted spoon, reserving the liquid. Strain the liquid into the tomatoes through a strainer lined with cheesecloth and simmer for an additional 15 minutes.

3. Meanwhile, heat 2 tablespoons of the olive oil in a heavy skillet. Add the chicken and cook, stirring frequently, for 3–4 minutes, until cooked through. Stir in the mushrooms and garlic and cook for an additional 5 minutes.

4. Bring a large saucepan of lightly salted water to a boil. Add the pasta, bring back to a boil, and cook for 8–10 minutes, or according to the package directions, until tender but still firm to the bite. Drain well, then transfer to a warm serving dish. Drizzle with the remaining olive oil and toss lightly. Stir the chicken mixture into the tomato sauce, season with salt and pepper, and spoon onto the pasta. Garnish with parsley and serve immediately.

Chicken Meatball Pasta

 SERVES 4   PREP TIME: 15 minutes   COOKING TIME: 35 minutes

nutritional information per serving	449 cal, 11g fat, 2g sat fat, 7g total sugars, 0.6g salt

This lighter, more delicately flavored twist on a familiar favorite is just as delicious and filling.

INGREDIENTS

3 tablespoons olive oil

1 red onion, chopped

14 ounces skinless, boneless chicken breasts, chopped

1 cup fresh white bread crumbs

2 teaspoons dried oregano

1 garlic clove, crushed

1 (14½-ounce) can diced tomatoes

1 tablespoon tomato paste

1¼ cups water

8 ounces dried spaghetti or linguine

salt and pepper

Parmesan cheese shavings, to serve

1. Heat 1 tablespoon of the oil in a large skillet and sauté half the chopped onion for 5 minutes, until just softened. Let cool.

2. Place the chicken, bread crumbs, oregano, and the fried onion in a food processor or blender. Season well with salt and pepper, then process for 2–3 minutes, until thoroughly combined. Shape into 24 meatballs.

3. Heat the remaining oil in the skillet and cook the meatballs over medium–high heat for 3–4 minutes, until golden brown. Remove and set aside.

4. Add the remaining onion and the garlic to the skillet and sauté for 5 minutes. Stir in the tomatoes, tomato paste, and water and bring to a boil. Add the meatballs and simmer for 20 minutes. Season with salt and pepper.

5. Meanwhile, bring a large saucepan of lightly salted water to a boil. Add the pasta, bring back to a boil, and cook for 8–10 minutes, or according to the package directions, until tender but still firm to the bite. Drain thoroughly and toss with the meatballs and sauce. Serve immediately with Parmesan cheese shavings.

Chicken with Creamy Penne

 SERVES 2   PREP TIME: 5 minutes   COOKING TIME: 10–15 minutes

nutritional information per serving	810 cal, 30g fat, 15g sat fat, 4g total sugars, 0.3g salt

It is the pure simplicity of this delicately flavored dish that makes it absolutely perfect.

INGREDIENTS

8 ounces dried penne

1 tablespoon olive oil

2 skinless, boneless chicken breasts

¼ cup dry white wine

¾ cup frozen peas

⅓ cup heavy cream

¼ cup chopped fresh parsley, to garnish

1. Bring a large saucepan of lightly salted water to a boil. Add the pasta, bring back to a boil, and cook for 8–10 minutes, or according to the package directions, until tender but still firm to the bite.

2. Meanwhile, heat the oil in a skillet, add the chicken, and cook over medium heat for about 4 minutes on each side, until cooked through and the juices run clear.

3. Pour in the wine and cook over high heat until it has almost evaporated.

4. Drain the pasta. Add the peas, cream, and pasta to the skillet and stir well. Cover and simmer for 2 minutes. Garnish with chopped parsley and serve immediately.

1

2
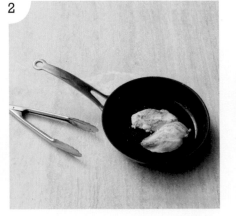

4

GOES WELL WITH
A colorful endive, orange, and beet salad with a yogurt dressing makes the perfect partner for this creamy dish.

Spaghetti with Parsley Chicken

 SERVES 4 · PREP TIME: 10 minutes · COOKING TIME: 35–40 minutes

nutritional information per serving	426 cal, 16g fat, 8g sat fat, 4g total sugars, 0.5g salt

Subtly spiced with a hint of citrus, this zingy dish is a good choice for easy, informal entertaining.

INGREDIENTS

1 tablespoon olive oil

thinly pared rind of 1 lemon, cut into julienne strips

1 teaspoon finely chopped fresh ginger

1 teaspoon sugar

1 cup chicken stock

8 ounces dried spaghetti

4 tablespoons butter

8 ounces skinless, boneless chicken breasts, diced

1 red onion, finely chopped

leaves from 2 bunches of flat-leaf parsley

salt

1. Heat the oil in a heavy saucepan. Add the lemon rind and cook over low heat, stirring frequently, for 5 minutes. Stir in the ginger and sugar, season with salt and cook, stirring continuously, for an additional 2 minutes. Pour in the stock, bring to a boil, then cook for 5 minutes, or until the liquid has reduced by half.

2. Meanwhile, bring a large saucepan of lightly salted water to a boil. Add the pasta, bring back to a boil, and cook for 8–10 minutes, or according to the package directions, until tender but still firm to the bite.

3. Melt half the butter in a skillet. Add the chicken and onion and cook, stirring frequently, for 5 minutes, or until cooked through and the juices run clear. Stir in the lemon and ginger mixture and cook for 1 minute. Stir in the parsley leaves and cook, stirring continuously, for an additional 3 minutes.

4. Drain the pasta and transfer to a warm serving dish, then add the remaining butter and toss well. Add the chicken sauce, toss again, and serve immediately.

Cajun Chicken Pasta

 SERVES 6

PREP TIME:
25 minutes

COOKING TIME:
30 minutes

nutritional information per serving	793 cal, 36g fat, 21g sat fat, 7.5g total sugars, 2.1g salt

Enjoy the spicy taste of New Orleans with this creamy mix of blackened chicken, pasta, and fresh-tasting vegetables.

INGREDIENTS

1¼ sticks butter

6 skinless boneless chicken breasts

3 tablespoons all-purpose flour

2 cups milk

1 cup light cream

6 scallions, chopped

1 pound dried pasta shapes, such as fusilli (corkscrew pasta) or farfalle (pasta bow ties)

½ cup grated Parmesan cheese

diced tomatoes and pitted ripe black olives, to garnish

spice mix

1 tablespoon sweet paprika

1½ teaspoons salt

1 teaspoon onion powder

1 teaspoon garlic powder

1 teaspoon dried thyme

1 teaspoon cayenne pepper

½ teaspoon black pepper

½ teaspoon dried oregano

1. Heat a cast-iron skillet over high heat until hot. Add 6 tablespoons of the butter and melt over low heat. Mix together all the spice mix ingredients in a shallow dish. Brush the chicken with the melted butter, dip into the spice mix to coat, shaking off the excess, and add to the skillet. Cook for 5–8 minutes on each side until speckled with black, then remove the skillet from the heat.

2. Meanwhile, melt 3 tablespoons of the remaining butter in a saucepan. Stir in the flour and cook, stirring continuously, for 1 minute. Remove the pan from the heat and beat in the milk and cream, then return to the heat and bring to a boil, beating continuously. Remove the pan from the heat.

3. Cut the chicken into chunks or thin strips and stir into the cream sauce with the scallions. Return the pan to medium–low heat and simmer, stirring frequently, for 20 minutes, until the chicken is cooked through.

4. Meanwhile, bring a large saucepan of lightly salted water to a boil. Add the pasta, bring back to a boil, and cook for 8–10 minutes, or according to the package directions, until tender but still firm to the bite. Drain, return to the pan, add the remaining butter and the cheese, and toss well, then transfer to a warm serving dish. Spoon the Cajun chicken on top, garnish with diced tomatoes and olives, and serve immediately.

Penne with Chicken & Feta Cheese

🍽 SERVES 4   👨‍🍳 PREP TIME: 10–15 minutes   ⏱ COOKING TIME: 25–30 minutes

nutritional information per serving	700 cal, 20g fat, 9g sat fat, 4g total sugars, 2.2g salt

The sharpness of the cheese gives a delicious piquancy to a dish that family and friends are sure to relish.

INGREDIENTS

2 tablespoons olive oil

1 pound skinless, boneless chicken breasts, cut into thin strips

6 scallions, chopped

1½ cups diced feta cheese

¼ cup snipped fresh chives

1 pound dried penne

salt and pepper

1. Heat the oil in a heavy skillet. Add the chicken and cook over medium heat, stirring frequently, for 5–8 minutes, or until cooked through. Add the scallions and cook for 2 minutes. Stir the feta cheese into the skillet with half the chives and season with salt and pepper.

2. Meanwhile, bring a large saucepan of lightly salted water to a boil. Add the pasta, bring back to a boil, and cook for 8–10 minutes, or according to the package directions, until tender but still firm to the bite. Drain thoroughly, then transfer to a warm serving dish.

3. Spoon the chicken mixture onto the pasta, toss lightly, and serve immediately, garnished with the remaining chives.

GOES WELL WITH

Why not keep the Greek theme and serve this dish with a fresh-tasting Greek salad of olives, tomatoes, and cucumber?

Pasta with Chicken & Bell Peppers

SERVES 4–6

PREP TIME:
25 minutes
plus marinating

COOKING TIME:
40 minutes

nutritional information per serving	500 cal, 11g fat, 2g sat fat, 8g total sugars, 0.4g salt

You have to allow time for the chicken to marinate, but this mouthwatering spicy dish is worth the wait.

INGREDIENTS

12 skinless, boneless chicken thighs, cubed
1 tablespoon peanut oil
1 red bell pepper, seeded and chopped
1 green bell pepper, seeded and chopped
1 cup can diced tomatoes
1 pound dried spaghetti
salt

marinade

2 tablespoons finely chopped scallions, plus extra to garnish
1–2 chiles, seeded and chopped
2 garlic cloves, finely chopped
1 teaspoon ground cinnamon
1 teaspoon ground allspice
pinch of grated nutmeg
2 teaspoons light brown sugar
2 tablespoons peanut oil
1 tablespoon lime juice
1 tablespoon white wine vinegar
salt and pepper

1. Put the chicken into a large, nonmetallic dish. Mix all the marinade ingredients in a bowl, mashing everything together. Spoon the mixture over the chicken and rub it in with your hands. Cover the dish with plastic wrap and let marinate in the refrigerator for at least 2 hours, preferably overnight.

2. Heat the oil in a saucepan, add the red bell pepper and green bell pepper, and cook over medium–low heat, stirring occasionally, for 5 minutes. Add the chicken and any remaining marinade and cook, stirring frequently, for 5 minutes, until cooked through. Add the tomatoes, reduce the heat, cover, and simmer, stirring occasionally, for 30 minutes. Check occasionally that the mixture is not drying out—if it is, add a little water.

3. Halfway through the chicken cooking time, bring a large saucepan of lightly salted water to a boil. Add the pasta, bring back to a boil, and cook for 8–10 minutes, or according to the package directions, until tender but still firm to the bite.

4. Drain the pasta, add it to the pan with the chicken and toss lightly. Transfer to warm plates, garnish with the scallion, and serve immediately.

Turkey & Pasta Soup

SERVES 4–6

PREP TIME:
15 minutes

COOKING TIME:
30–35 minutes

nutritional information
per serving   273 cal, 3g fat, 0.5g sat fat, 4.5g total sugars, 1g salt

This quick and easy, colorful bowlful of pure comfort food is a great way to use up leftover turkey.

INGREDIENTS

1 tablespoon olive oil

1 large onion, chopped

2 carrots, chopped

2 celery stalks, chopped

8¾ cups chicken stock or turkey stock

2 cups shredded, cooked turkey

6 ounces dried spaghetti, cooked

salt and pepper

1. Heat the oil in a large saucepan, add the onion, carrots, and celery, and cook over low heat, stirring occasionally, for 8–10 minutes, until the onion is just starting to brown.

2. Pour in the stock, increase the heat to medium, and bring to a boil. Reduce the heat, season with salt and pepper, and simmer for 15 minutes.

3. Add the turkey and cooked spaghetti, stir well, and simmer for an additional 5 minutes. Taste and adjust the seasoning, if necessary, then ladle into warm bowls and serve immediately.

FREEZING TIP
If you have more turkey, double the quantity and freeze half before adding the pasta. Store for up to one month and thaw at room temperature.

Turkey Tetrazzini

 SERVES 4–6   PREP TIME: 15 minutes   COOKING TIME: 35–40 minutes

nutritional information per serving	600 cal, 31g fat, 16g sat fat, 2g total sugars, 1g salt

Named after a famous opera singer, this fabulous dish would certainly have a starring role when you're entertaining guests.

INGREDIENTS

3 tablespoons olive oil

1½ pounds turkey breast cutlets, diced

1 stick butter, plus extra for greasing

2 tablespoons all-purpose flour

2 cups chicken stock

dash of Tabasco sauce

1 egg yolk

2 tablespoons medium sherry

½ cup light cream

8 ounces dried tagliatelle

3 cups sliced white button mushrooms

⅔ cup freshly grated Parmesan cheese

1 cup fresh bread crumbs

salt

1. Heat the oil in a skillet, add the turkey, and cook over medium heat, stirring frequently, for 8–10 minutes, until cooked through. Remove from the heat.

2. Melt half the butter in a saucepan, stir in the flour, and cook, stirring continuously, for 1 minute. Remove from the heat and gradually stir in the stock. Return to the heat and bring to a boil, stirring continuously. Boil for 1 minute, until thickened and smooth, then stir in the Tabasco sauce, season with salt, and remove from the heat.

3. Beat the egg yolk with a fork in a bowl, then beat in 2 tablespoons of the hot sauce. Stir the mixture into the sauce in the pan, then stir in the sherry, cream, and turkey. Return the pan to low heat and heat through, stirring continuously, but do not boil. Remove the pan from the heat.

4. Bring a large saucepan of lightly salted water to a boil. Add the pasta, bring back to a boil, and cook for 8–10 minutes, or according to the package directions, until tender but still firm to the bite. Meanwhile, melt half the remaining butter in a small saucepan, add the mushrooms, and cook, stirring occasionally, for 4–5 minutes. Add the mushrooms to the turkey mixture.

5. Preheat the broiler. Grease a flameproof casserole dish with butter. Drain the pasta. Make alternating layers of the turkey mixture and pasta in the dish. Sprinkle with the grated cheese and bread crumbs, dot with the remaining butter, and cook under the preheated broiler until the top is golden and bubbling. Serve immediately.

Jumbo Pasta Shells with Turkey

 SERVES 4 PREP TIME: 15 minutes COOKING TIME: 50 minutes

nutritional information per serving	724 cal, 24g fat, 10g sat fat, 5g total sugars, 0.9g salt

This is a delicious way to serve stuffed pasta without having to spend time making fresh pasta dough.

INGREDIENTS

2 cups tomato puree

16 jumbo dried pasta shells

3 tablespoons olive oil

1 onion, finely chopped

2 garlic cloves, finely chopped

1 pound fresh ground turkey

1 tablespoon tomato paste

1 tablespoon finely chopped fresh flat-leaf parsley

8 ounces mozzarella cheese, shredded

1–2 teaspoons black olive paste

salt and pepper

1. Pour the tomato puree into a nylon strainer set over a bowl and set aside. Bring a large saucepan of lightly salted water to a boil. Add the pasta, bring back to a boil, and cook for 8–10 minutes, or according to the package directions, until tender but still firm to the bite. Drain and set aside. Preheat the oven to 350°F.

2. Meanwhile, heat 2 tablespoons of the oil in a skillet, add the onion and half the garlic, and cook over low heat, stirring occasionally, for 5 minutes, until soft. Add the turkey, increase the heat to medium, and cook, stirring occasionally, for 8–10 minutes, until cooked through. Stir in the tomato paste, parsley, and half the cheese, season with salt and pepper, and remove the pan from the heat.

3. Put the strained tomato puree into a bowl and stir in the olive paste and the remaining oil and garlic. Spread half of this mixture over the bottom of a casserole dish. Divide the turkey mixture among the pasta shells and put them in the dish, meat-side up, then pour the remaining tomato puree mixture over them. Cover the dish with aluminum foil and bake in the preheated oven for 25 minutes.

4. Remove the dish from the oven and discard the foil. Sprinkle the remaining cheese over the pasta, return the dish to the oven, and bake for an additional 5 minutes, until the cheese has melted. Serve immediately.

Turkey Pasta Primavera

 SERVES 4   PREP TIME: 5 minutes   COOKING TIME: 30–40 minutes

nutritional information **per serving**	818 cal, 41g fat, 22g sat fat, 7g total sugars, 0.6g salt

Primavera means "spring" and this is a fabulous way to make the most of the fresh, young vegetables in season.

INGREDIENTS

2 tablespoons butter
2 tablespoons olive oil
2 shallots, finely chopped
1 garlic clove, finely chopped
1 pound diced turkey
4 ounces asparagus tips
2 carrots, thinly sliced diagonally
1½ cups sliced button mushrooms
1 tablespoon chopped fresh sage
1 tablespoon chopped fresh flat-leaf parsley
⅔ cup dry white wine
¾ cup heavy cream
10 ounces dried pasta shapes, such as farfalle (pasta bow ties)
⅔ cup freshly grated Parmesan cheese
salt and pepper

1. Melt the butter with the oil in a large skillet, add the shallots and garlic, and cook over low heat, stirring occasionally, for 3–4 minutes, until soft. Add the turkey, increase the heat to medium, and cook, stirring frequently, for 6–8 minutes, until cooked through.

2. Add the asparagus tips, carrots, and mushrooms and cook, gently stirring occasionally, for 4–5 minutes, until starting to soften, then add the herbs, wine, and cream. Reduce the heat and simmer stirring occasionally, for 10–15 minutes, until the vegetables are tender.

3. Meanwhile, bring a large saucepan of lightly salted water to a boil. Add the pasta, bring back to a boil, and cook for 8–10 minutes, or according to the package directions, until tender but still firm to the bite. Drain the pasta, transfer to the pan of sauce, season with salt and pepper, and toss well. Transfer to a warm serving dish, sprinkle with the cheese, and serve immediately.

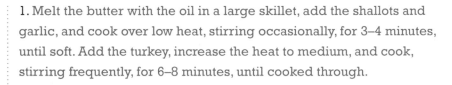

SOMETHING
DIFFERENT
This recipe has
almost infinite
variations—just
substitute your
favorite vegetables
and herbs.

Pasta with Chile Barbecue Sauce

SERVES 4   PREP TIME: 20 minutes   COOKING TIME: 30 minutes

nutritional information
per serving   726 cal, 21g fat, 6g sat fat, 24g total sugars, 1.2g salt

Even if it's pouring with rain outside, you can enjoy a touch of summer with this spicy barbecue-style pasta sauce.

INGREDIENTS

2 tablespoons olive oil

2 garlic cloves, finely chopped

1 large onion, finely chopped

2 red bell peppers, seeded and chopped

1–2 chiles, seeded and finely chopped

1 pound fresh ground turkey

1 (11-ounce) can corn kernels, drained

1 quantity Basic Tomato Sauce (see page 272)

2 tablespoons Worcestershire sauce

1 tablespoon red wine vinegar

1 tablespoon light brown sugar

12 ounces dried fusilli

2 tablespoons chopped fresh parsley

salt and pepper

pickled chiles, drained and sliced, to garnish (optional)

1. Heat the oil in a skillet, add the garlic, onion, red bell peppers, and chiles, and cook over low heat, stirring occasionally, for 5 minutes. Increase the heat to medium, add the turkey, and cook, stirring frequently, for 5–8 minutes, until cooked through.

2. Stir in the corn, tomato sauce, Worcestershire sauce, vinegar, and sugar. Season with salt and pepper and simmer for 15 minutes.

3. Meanwhile, bring a large saucepan of lightly salted water to a boil. Add the pasta, bring back to a boil, and cook for 8–10 minutes, or according to the package directions, until tender but still firm to the bite. Drain and transfer to the pan of sauce. Add the parsley, taste, and adjust the seasoning, if necessary, and remove from the heat. Transfer to a warm serving dish and serve immediately, garnished with the pickled chiles, if using.

1

2

2

FREEZING TIP
You can freeze the sauce in an airtight container for up to two months, so why not make double the quantity?

Pasta with Harissa Turkey Meatballs

SERVES 4   PREP TIME: 15 minutes   COOKING TIME: 15–20 minutes

nutritional information per serving	560 cal, 10g fat, 3g sat fat, 7.5g total sugars, 0.7g salt

If you like spicy food, this North African-style dish is the perfect choice, and you can easily adjust the heat to suit you.

INGREDIENTS

12 ounces fresh ground turkey

½ cup dry bread crumbs

⅓ cup Greek-style yogurt

1 egg

½ teaspoon ground coriander

½ teaspoon ground cumin

½–1 teaspoon harissa

3 tablespoons finely chopped parsley

12 ounces dried spaghetti or tagliatelle

olive oil, for drizzling

salt and pepper

sauce

1 (14½-ounce) can diced tomatoes

1 small chile, seeded and finely chopped

¼ teaspoon ground cinnamon

½ teaspoon ground cumin

1. Preheat the oven to 400°F and line a baking sheet with parchment paper.

2. Mix together the turkey, bread crumbs, yogurt, egg, coriander, cumin, harissa, and parsley in a bowl until thoroughly combined. Season with salt and pepper. Shape the mixture into meatballs about the size of a golf ball and put them on the prepared baking sheet. Bake for 15 minutes, until lightly browned.

3. Meanwhile, bring a large saucepan of lightly salted water to a boil. Add the pasta, bring back to a boil, and cook for 8–10 minutes, or according to the package directions, until tender but still firm to the bite. Drain, transfer to a warm dish, drizzle with oil, and toss to coat.

4. Meanwhile, put all the sauce ingredients into a saucepan and simmer, stirring occasionally, for 5 minutes, until thickened.

5. Remove the meatballs from the oven and add to the pasta. Pour the sauce over them and toss together. Serve immediately.

Fettuccine with Duck Sauce

SERVES 4   PREP TIME: 15 minutes   COOKING TIME: 1¾ hours

nutritional information per serving	768 cal, 27g fat, 6g sat fat, 10g total sugars, 1.3g salt

This unmistakably special occasion dish comes from northern Italy and makes a good choice for a celebration meal.

INGREDIENTS

¼ cup olive oil

4 duck legs

1 shallot, finely chopped

1 leek, white part only, finely chopped

1 garlic clove, finely chopped

1 celery stalk, finely chopped

1 carrot, finely chopped

4 pancetta or bacon slices, diced

1 tablespoon finely chopped fresh flat-leaf parsley

1 bay leaf

⅓ cup dry white wine

1 (14½-ounce) can diced tomatoes

2 tablespoons tomato paste

pinch of sugar

1 pound dried fettuccine

salt and pepper

freshly grated Parmesan cheese, to serve

1. Heat half the oil in a skillet. Add the duck and cook over medium heat, turning frequently, for 8–10 minutes, until golden brown. Using a slotted spoon, transfer to a large saucepan.

2. Wipe out the skillet with paper towels, then add the remaining oil. Add the shallot, leek, garlic, celery, carrot, and pancetta and cook over low heat, stirring, for 10 minutes. Using a slotted spoon, transfer the mixture to the skillet with the duck and stir in the parsley. Add the bay leaf and season with salt and pepper. Pour in the wine and cook over high heat, stirring occasionally, until reduced by half. Add the tomatoes, tomato paste, and sugar and cook for an additional 5 minutes. Pour in just enough water to cover and bring to a boil. Lower the heat, cover, and simmer gently for 1 hour, until the duck is cooked through and tender.

3. Remove the skillet from the heat and transfer the duck to a cutting board. Skim off the fat from the surface of the sauce and discard the bay leaf. Remove and discard the skin from the duck and cut the meat off the bones, then dice. Return the duck meat to the skillet and keep warm.

4. Bring a large saucepan of lightly salted water to a boil. Add the pasta, bring back to a boil, and cook for 8–10 minutes, or according to the package direcions, until tender but still firm to the bite. Drain and place in a serving dish, then spoon the duck sauce over the pasta. Sprinkle generously with Parmesan cheese and serve immediately.

Venetian Duck with Spaghetti

 SERVES 4   PREP TIME: 20 minutes   COOKING TIME: 2 hours

nutritional information per serving	600 cal, 16g fat, 5.5g sat fat, 3.5g total sugars, 0.4g salt

This is a simpler version of a traditional dish made with bigoli—thick spaghetti made with flour, butter, and duck eggs—and preserved duck.

INGREDIENTS

4 duck legs
1 tablespoon duck fat
1 tablespoon butter
1 pound dried spaghetti
3 garlic cloves, peeled
juice and grated rind of ½ lemon
salt and pepper

1. Preheat the oven to 300°F. Prick the skin on the duck legs all over with a metal skewer or the tip of a sharp knife and season well with salt. Put in a small roasting pan or ovenproof dish, fitting them snugly in a single layer. Roast in the preheated oven for 1½ hours, then increase the oven temperature to 400°F and roast for an additional 15 minutes, until the skin is light golden and crisp. Remove from the oven and let cool.

2. Remove the skin from the duck legs and coarsely chop, then remove all the meat and coarsely chop.

3. Heat a heavy saucepan over medium heat, add the duck skin and meat with the duck fat and butter, and cook over medium–low heat for 10–12 minutes.

4. Meanwhile, bring a large saucepan of lightly salted water to a boil. Add the pasta, bring back to a boil, and cook for 8–10 minutes, or according to the package directions, until tender but still firm to the bite.

5. Add the garlic to the pan with the duck and cook, stirring occasionally, for a few minutes, until the garlic starts to brown, then remove the pan from the heat. Remove and discard the garlic. Drain the pasta, add to the pan, and return the pan to medium heat. Toss together, then add the lemon juice, season with pepper, and toss again. Transfer to a warm serving dish, sprinkle with the lemon rind, and serve immediately.

Salad Niçoise *118*

Spaghetti with Tuna & Parsley *120*

Spaghetti with Tuna Sauce *122*

Penne all'Arrabbiata with Smoked Cod *124*

Spaghetti & Cod *126*

Fettuccine with Sole & Monkfish *128*

Fusilli with Smoked Salmon & Dill *130*

Tagliatelle with Smoked Salmon & Arugula *132*

Sicilian Swordfish Pasta *134*

Linguine with Anchovies, Olives & Capers *136*

Linguine with Sardines *138*

Pasta Salad with Melon & Shrimp *140*

Fettuccine & Shrimp Packages *142*

Artichoke & Shrimp Rigatoni *144*

Garlic Shrimp with Angel-hair Pasta *146*

Linguine with Shrimp & Scallops *148*

Fusilli With Cajun Seafood Sauce *150*

Scallop Soup with Pasta *152*

Linguine with Clams in Tomato Sauce *154*

Penne with Squid & Tomatoes *156*

Mussel & Pasta Soup *158*

Conchiglie with Mussels *160*

Ravioli with Crabmeat & Ricotta *162*

Farfallini Buttered Lobster *164*

Fish & Seafood

Salad Niçoise

nutritional information per serving	405 cal, 14g fat, 3g sat fat, 4g total sugars, 1.2g salt

It is a matter of debate in culinary circles whether this Mediterranean salad should contain tomatoes, green beans, or hard-boiled eggs, but most renditions contain all these ingredients.

INGREDIENTS

12 ounces dried conchiglie

2 tuna steaks, about ¾ inch thick

olive oil, for brushing

2 cups trimmed green beans

store-bought garlic vinaigrette, to taste

2 hearts of lettuce, leaves separated

3 extra-large hard-boiled eggs, halved

2 juicy tomatoes, cut into wedges

1 (2-ounce) anchovy fillets in oil, drained

½ cup pitted ripe black olives or Niçoise olives

salt and pepper

1. Bring a large saucepan of lightly salted water to a boil. Add the pasta, bring back to a boil, and cook for 8–10 minutes, or according to the package directions, until tender but still firm to the bite. Drain and refresh in cold water.

2. Heat a ridged, cast-iron grill pan over high heat. Brush the tuna steaks with oil on one side, place oiled-side down on the hot pan, and chargrill for 2 minutes.

3. Lightly brush the top side of the tuna steaks with a little more oil. Turn the tuna steaks over, then season with salt and pepper. Continue chargrilling for an additional 2 minutes for rare or up to 4 minutes for well done. Let cool.

4. Meanwhile, bring a large saucepan of lightly salted water to a boil. Add the beans and return to a boil, then boil for 3 minutes. Drain and immediately transfer to a large bowl. Pour the garlic vinaigrette over the beans and stir together.

5. To serve, line a large serving plate with lettuce leaves. Lift the beans out of the bowl, leaving the excess dressing behind, and pile them in the center of the plate. Break the tuna into large flakes and arrange it over the beans. Arrange the hard-boiled eggs, tomatoes, anchovy fillets, and olives on the plate. Drizzle with more vinaigrette, if required, and serve immediately.

Spaghetti with Tuna & Parsley

SERVES 4

PREP TIME: 10 minutes

COOKING TIME: 15 minutes

nutritional information per serving	1,109 cal, 70g fat, 21g sat fat, 5g total sugars, 1.6g salt

This tasty dish is a great pantry standby that can be rustled up in no time at all.

INGREDIENTS

1 pound dried spaghetti

2 tablespoons butter

1 (5-ounce) can chunk light tuna in spring water, drained

1 (2-ounce) can anchovies, drained

1¼ cups olive oil

1 large bunch of fresh flat-leaf parsley, coarsely chopped

⅔ cup crème fraîche or sour cream

salt and pepper

1. Bring a large saucepan of lightly salted water to a boil. Add the pasta, bring back to a boil, and cook for 8–10 minutes, or according to the package directions, until tender but still firm to the bite. Drain the spaghetti in a colander and return to the pan. Add the butter, toss thoroughly to coat, and keep warm until required.

2. Flake the tuna into smaller pieces using two forks. Place the tuna in a food processor or blender with the anchovies, oil, and parsley and process until the sauce is smooth. Pour in the crème fraîche and process for a few seconds to blend. Taste the sauce and season with salt and pepper, if necessary.

3. Shake the pan of spaghetti over medium heat for a few minutes, or until it is thoroughly warm.

4. Pour the sauce over the spaghetti and toss. Serve immediately.

GOES WELL WITH
A mixed bean
salad, perhaps
including some
fresh green
beans, would be
a perfect match
for this dish.

Spaghetti with Tuna Sauce

 SERVES 4   PREP TIME: 10 minutes   COOKING TIME: 15 minutes

nutritional information per serving	493 cal, 8g fat, 1g sat fat, 8g total sugars, 0.8g salt

This is a terrific standby dish for those times when you have run out of ideas or are simply feeling tired.

INGREDIENTS

12 ounces dried spaghetti

2 tablespoons olive oil

1 garlic clove, peeled

1 onion, chopped

4 tomatoes, chopped

3 (5-ounce) cans chunk light tuna in spring water, drained and flaked

2 tablespoons capers, rinsed (optional)

2 tablespoons chopped fresh parsley, or 1 tablespoon chopped fresh basil, or a pinch of dried oregano

salt and pepper

1. Bring a large saucepan of lightly salted water to a boil. Add the pasta, bring back to a boil, and cook for 8–10 minutes, or according to the package directions, until tender but still firm to the bite.

2. Meanwhile, heat the oil in a separate saucepan and add the garlic. When it has begun to brown, remove and discard it. Add the onion and tomatoes to the pan and cook over low heat, stirring occasionally, for 5 minutes.

3. Drain the pasta and transfer to the pan with the vegetables. Add the tuna and capers, if using, and toss over the heat for a few minutes, until heated through. Remove from the heat, season with salt and pepper, stir in the herbs, and serve immediately.

SOMETHING
DIFFERENT
You can add extra
ingredients, such
as a few chopped
canned anchovies or
sliced, pitted olives,
depending on what
you have at hand.

Penne all'Arrabbiata with Smoked Cod

SERVES 4–6

PREP TIME:
15 minutes

COOKING TIME:
25 minutes

nutritional information per serving	375 cal, 13g fat, 2g sat fat, 3.5g total sugars, 2.1g salt

Arrabbiata means "angry" and describes the fierce heat from the local chiles in this dish from the Lazio region of Italy.

INGREDIENTS

⅓ cup olive oil

2 garlic cloves, finely chopped

2–3 dried chiles, finely chopped

4 tomatoes, chopped

10 ounces dried penne

1½ pounds cod fillets, skinned and cut into large chunks

2 tablespoons chopped fresh flat-leaf parsley

salt

1. Heat the oil in a large saucepan, add the garlic and chiles, and cook over low heat, stirring occasionally, for a few minutes, until the garlic is beginning to brown. Stir in the tomatoes, season with salt, and simmer for 15 minutes.

2. Bring a large saucepan of lightly salted water to a boil. Add the pasta, bring back to a boil, and cook for 8–10 minutes, or according to the package directions, until tender but still firm to the bite.

3. Meanwhile, add the chunks of fish to the sauce, gently stir, and simmer for an additional 10 minutes.

4. Drain the pasta, transfer to the sauce, and add the parsley. Toss together. Spoon into warm bowls and serve immediately.

1

1

3

COOK'S NOTE
It's important that
the tomatoes are
sweet and ripe,
so if they're not in
season, substitute
2 cups of canned
crushed tomatoes.

Spaghetti & Cod

 SERVES 4

PREP TIME:
10 minutes

COOKING TIME:
12 minutes

nutritional information
per serving
725 cal, 39g fat, 6g sat fat, 6g total sugars, 0.3g salt

*This recipe is incredibly quick and easy to prepare,
and the dish is surprisingly tasty.*

INGREDIENTS

10 ounces dried spaghetti

1 cup extra virgin olive oil

1 garlic clove, peeled

3 cups halved cherry tomatoes

pinch of crushed red peppers
(optional)

1¼ pounds cod fillets, skinned
and cut into small chunks

salt and pepper

1. Bring a large saucepan of lightly salted water to a boil. Add the pasta, bring back to a boil, and cook for 8–10 minutes, or according to the package directions, until tender but still firm to the bite. Reserve.

2. Meanwhile, put the oil into a large saucepan, add the garlic, and cook over low heat, stirring occasionally, for a few minutes, until the garlic starts to brown, then remove and discard. Add the tomatoes to the pan and season with salt. Increase the heat to high and cook, tossing occasionally, for 6–7 minutes, until lightly browned and concentrated without disintegrating.

3. Add the crushed red peppers, if using, and the fish and cook, stirring gently, for 1–2 minutes. Add a ladleful of the cooking water from the pasta and taste and adjust the seasoning, if necessary. Drain the pasta, add it to the sauce, and toss together. Remove from the heat, spoon into warm bowls, and serve immediately.

SOMETHING DIFFERENT

You can substitute another firm-fleshed white fish, such as halibut or red snapper for the cod.

Fettuccine with Sole & Monkfish

SERVES 4

PREP TIME:
15 minutes

COOKING TIME:
50 minutes

nutritional information per serving	877 cal, 23g fat, 12g sat fat, 8.5g total sugars, 1.3g salt

This is a wonderful dish not just for those who love fish but also for anyone who loves good food.

INGREDIENTS

1 pound lemon sole fillets

1 pound monkfish fillets

⅔ cup all-purpose flour

6 tablespoons unsalted butter

4 shallots, finely chopped

2 garlic cloves, crushed

1 carrot, diced

1 leek, finely chopped

1¼ cups fish stock

1¼ cups dry white wine

2 teaspoons anchovy extract

1 tablespoon balsamic vinegar

1 pound dried fettuccine

salt and pepper

chopped fresh flat-leaf parsley, to garnish

1. Skin the lemon sole and monkfish fillets and cut into equal chunks.

2. Season the flour with salt and pepper and spread out 2 tablespoons of the mixture on a plate. Coat all the fish pieces with it, shaking off the excess. Melt the butter in a heavy saucepan or flameproof casserole dish. Add the fish, shallots, garlic, carrot, and leek and cook over low heat, stirring frequently, for 10 minutes. Sprinkle in the remaining seasoned flour and cook, stirring continuously, for 1 minute.

3. Mix together the fish stock, wine, anchovy extract, and balsamic vinegar in a small bowl and gradually stir into the fish mixture. Bring to a boil, stirring continuously, then reduce the heat and simmer gently for 35 minutes.

4. Meanwhile, bring a large saucepan of lightly salted water to a boil. Add the pasta, bring back to a boil, and cook for 8–10 minutes, or according to the package directions, until tender but still firm to the bite. Drain and transfer to a warm serving dish. Spoon the fish mixture onto the pasta, garnish with chopped parsley, and serve immediately.

Fusilli with Smoked Salmon & Dill

SERVES 4

PREP TIME:
10 minutes

COOKING TIME:
25–30 minutes

nutritional information per serving	1,143 cal, 76g fat, 44g sat fat, 5g total sugars, 2g salt

This is not a traditional combination, but pasta and smoked salmon is now fashionable in restaurants in Italy's capital city of Rome.

INGREDIENTS

1 pound dried fusilli

4 tablespoons unsalted butter

1 small onion, finely chopped

⅓ cup dry white wine

2 cups heavy cream

8 ounces smoked salmon

2 tablespoons snipped fresh dill, plus extra sprigs to garnish

1–2 tablespoons lemon juice

salt and pepper

crusty bread, to serve

1. Bring a large saucepan of lightly salted water to a boil. Add the pasta, bring back to a boil, and cook for 8–10 minutes, or according to the package directions, until tender but still firm to the bite.

2. Meanwhile, melt the butter in a heavy saucepan. Add the onion and cook over low heat, stirring occasionally, for 5 minutes, or until softened. Add the wine, bring to a boil, and continue boiling until reduced by two-thirds. Pour in the cream and season with salt and pepper. Bring to a boil, reduce the heat, and simmer for 2 minutes, or until slightly thickened. Cut the smoked salmon into squares and stir into the pan with the snipped dill and lemon juice to taste.

3. Drain the pasta and transfer to a warm serving dish. Add the smoked salmon mixture and toss well. Garnish with dill sprigs and serve immediately with the crusty bread.

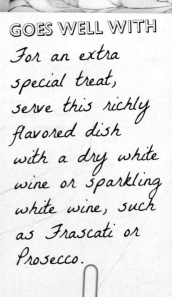

GOES WELL WITH

For an extra special treat, serve this richly flavored dish with a dry white wine or sparkling white wine, such as Frascati or Prosecco.

Tagliatelle with Smoked Salmon & Arugula

SERVES 4

PREP TIME:
5 minutes

COOKING TIME:
15 minutes

nutritional information
per serving

1,141 cal, 76g fat, 44g sat fat, 5g total sugars, 2g salt

This must be one of the easiest dishes to prepare— and one of the most delicious to eat.

INGREDIENTS

12 ounces dried tagliatelle

2 tablespoons olive oil

1 garlic clove, finely chopped

4 ounces smoked salmon, cut into thin strips

3 cups arugula

salt and pepper

1. Bring a large saucepan of lightly salted water to a boil. Add the pasta, bring back to a boil, and cook for 8–10 minutes, or according to the package directions, until tender but still firm to the bite.

2. Just before the end of the cooking time, heat the olive oil in a heavy skillet. Add the garlic and cook over low heat, stirring continuously, for 1 minute. Do not let the garlic brown or it will taste bitter.

3. Add the salmon and arugula. Season with pepper and cook, stirring continuously, for 1 minute. Remove the skillet from the heat.

4. Drain the pasta and transfer to a warm serving dish. Add the smoked salmon and arugula mixture, toss lightly and serve immediately.

GOES WELL WITH
Garlic bread would
make a wonderful
complement without
detracting from the
delicate flavors
of the dish.

Sicilian Swordfish Pasta

 SERVES 4 PREP TIME: 20 minutes COOKING TIME: 30 minutes

nutritional information per serving	441 cal, 10g fat, 2g sat fat, 6.5g total sugars, 1.1g salt

Sicily is famous for its swordfish recipes, which often also include other favorite ingredients, such as capers and olives.

INGREDIENTS

1 tablespoon olive oil

4 garlic cloves, peeled

1 onion, chopped

8 ripe black olives, pitted and chopped

4 small pickles, chopped

2 tablespoons capers in salt, rinsed and chopped

10 ounces dried spaghetti or linguine

1 (14½-ounce) can diced tomatoes

1 pound swordfish, cut into small chunks

basil leaves, to garnish

salt and pepper

1. Heat the oil in a deep skillet and add the garlic. When the garlic begins to brown, remove and discard. Add the onion and cook over low heat, stirring occasionally, for 8–10 minutes, until light golden. Stir in the olives, pickles, and capers, season with salt and pepper, and cook, stirring occasionally, for 5 minutes.

2. Meanwhile, bring a large saucepan of lightly salted water to a boil. Add the pasta, bring back to a boil, and cook for 8–10 minutes, or according to the package directions, until tender but still firm to the bite.

3. Add the tomatoes to the skillet, increase the heat to medium, and bring to a boil, stirring occasionally, then reduce the heat and simmer for 5 minutes. Add the swordfish chunks, cover, and simmer gently for an additional 5 minutes.

4. Drain the pasta and transfer to a warm serving dish. Top with the swordfish sauce, tear the basil leaves and sprinkle over the fish, and serve immediately.

COOK'S NOTE

Although it's an oily fish, swordfish dries out easily, so simmer until it is just opaque to avoid overcooking.

Linguine with Anchovies, Olives & Capers

|O| SERVES 4   PREP TIME: 10 minutes   COOKING TIME: 30 minutes

nutritional information per serving	511 cal, 17g fat, 2.5g sat fat, 5g total sugars, 1.6g salt

This quick and easy dish has all the characteristics of a great Southern Italian meal—piquant chiles, beautiful black olives, and luscious tomatoes.

INGREDIENTS

3 tablespoons olive oil

2 garlic cloves, finely chopped

10 anchovy fillets, drained and chopped

1½ cups ripe black olives, pitted and chopped

1 tablespoon capers, rinsed

7 plum tomatoes, peeled, seeded, and chopped

1 pound dried linguine

salt and cayenne pepper

2 tablespoons chopped fresh flat-leaf parsley, to garnish

1. Heat the oil in a heavy saucepan. Add the garlic and cook over low heat, stirring frequently, for 2 minutes. Add the anchovies and mash them to a pulp with a fork.

2. Add the olives, capers, and tomatoes and season with cayenne pepper. Cover and simmer for 25 minutes.

3. Meanwhile, bring a saucepan of lightly salted water to a boil. Add the pasta, bring back to a boil, and cook for 8–10 minutes, or according to the package directions, until tender but still firm to the bite.

4. Drain the pasta and transfer to a warm serving dish. Spoon the anchovy sauce over the pasta and toss. Garnish with chopped parsley and serve immediately.

1

2

3

Linguine with Sardines

 SERVES 4   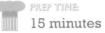 PREP TIME: 15 minutes   COOKING TIME: 25–30 minutes

nutritional information per serving	624 cal, 27g fat, 5g sat fat, 3g total sugars, 0.3g salt

This classic Sicilian dish with its robust flavors is filling, delicious and a great addition to a healthy diet.

INGREDIENTS

8 sardines, filleted, washed and dried

¼ cup olive oil

3 garlic cloves, sliced

1 teaspoon crushed red pepper

1 fennel bulb, trimmed and thinly sliced

12 ounces dried linguine

½ teaspoon finely grated lemon rind

1 tablespoon lemon juice

2 tablespoons toasted pine nuts

2 tablespoons chopped fresh parsley

salt and pepper

1. Coarsely chop the sardines into large pieces and reserve.

2. Heat 2 tablespoons of the oil in a large skillet over medium–high heat and add the garlic and crushed red pepper. Cook for 1 minute, then add the fennel. Cook, stirring occasionally, for 4–5 minutes, or until soft. Reduce the heat, add the sardine pieces, and cook for an additional 3–4 minutes.

3. Meanwhile, bring a large saucepan of lightly salted water to a boil. Add the pasta, bring back to a boil, and cook for 8–10 minutes, or according to the package directions, until tender but still firm to the bite. Drain thoroughly and return to the pan.

4. Add the lemon rind, lemon juice, pine nuts, and parsley to the sardine mixture and toss. Season with salt and pepper.

5. Add to the pasta with the remaining oil and toss. Transfer to a warm serving dish and serve immediately.

Artichoke & Shrimp Rigatoni

 SERVES 4

PREP TIME:
15 minutes

COOKING TIME:
25–30 minutes

nutritional information per serving	611 cal, 27g fat, 7g sat fat, 6g total sugars, 0.4g salt

Globe artichokes grow wild in Sicily and are cultivated throughout Italy, but they are always considered a speciality of recipes from Rome.

INGREDIENTS

2 tablespoons lemon juice

4 baby globe artichokes

½ cup olive oil

2 shallots, finely chopped

2 garlic cloves, finely chopped

2 tablespoons chopped fresh
flat-leaf parsley

2 tablespoons chopped fresh mint

12 ounces dried rigatoni

2 tablespoons unsalted butter

12 large shrimp,
peeled and deveined

salt and pepper

1. Fill a bowl with cold water and add the lemon juice. Prepare the artichokes one at a time. Cut off the stems and trim away any tough outer leaves. Cut across the tops of the leaves. Slice in half lengthwise and remove the fibrous chokes in the center, then cut lengthwise into ¼-inch thick slices. Immediately place the slices in the bowl of acidulated water to prevent discoloration.

2. Heat ⅓ cup of the oil in a heavy skillet. Drain the artichoke slices and pat dry with paper towels. Add them to the skillet with the shallots, garlic, parsley, and mint and cook over low heat, stirring frequently, for 10–12 minutes, until tender.

3. Meanwhile, bring a large saucepan of lightly salted water to a boil. Add the pasta, bring back to a boil, and cook for 8–10 minutes, or according to the package directions, until tender but still firm to the bite.

4. Melt the butter in a small skillet and add the shrimp. Cook, stirring occasionally, for 2–3 minutes, until opaque and firm to the touch. Season with salt and pepper.

5. Drain the pasta and transfer to a bowl. Add the remaining oil and toss. Add the artichoke mixture and the shrimp and toss again. Spoon into warm bowls and serve immediately.

Garlic Shrimp with Angel-Hair Pasta

 SERVES 4   PREP TIME: 25 minutes   COOKING TIME: 45 minutes

nutritional information per serving	593 cal, 21g fat, 4g sat fat, 4g total sugars, 0.6g salt

Truly a dish made in heaven, this is a special treat for a celebration and is ideal for easy—and impressive—entertaining.

INGREDIENTS

1 pound jumbo shrimp

1 avocado

2 tablespoons lemon juice

¼ cup olive oil

1 onion, finely chopped

1½ cups dry white wine

1 bouquet garni

10 ounces dried angel-hair pasta

3 large garlic cloves, finely chopped

salt and pepper

1. Peel the shrimp, reserving the heads and shells. Cut along the back of each shrimp and remove the black vein. Peel, pit, and slice the avocado, put into a bowl, and toss with the lemon juice.

2. Heat half the oil in a saucepan, add the onion, and cook over low heat, stirring occasionally, for 5 minutes. Add the shrimp heads and shells and cook, mashing with a wooden spoon, for 5 minutes, then add the wine and bouquet garni. Increase the heat to medium and bring to a boil. Reduce the heat and simmer for 20 minutes.

3. Meanwhile, bring a large saucepan of lightly salted water to a boil. Add the pasta, bring back to a boil, and cook for 3 minutes. Remove from the heat, drain, and set aside.

4. Remove and discard the bouquet garni. Transfer the shrimp shell mixture to a food processor or blender and process until combined, then strain into a clean saucepan. Bring to a boil, then add the pasta and cook for a few more minutes, until the pasta is tender but still firm to the bite.

5. Meanwhile, heat the remaining oil in a skillet over medium heat. Add the shrimp and cook, stirring frequently, for 2–3 minutes, until opaque and firm to the touch. Add the garlic and cook, stirring frequently for an additional minute. Season with salt and pepper and remove from the heat.

6. Drain the pasta, toss with the avocado, and transfer to a serving dish. Top with the shrimp and serve immediately.

Linguine with Shrimp & Scallops

SERVES 6   PREP TIME: 15 minutes   COOKING TIME: 25–30 minutes

nutritional information per serving	514 cal, 10g fat, 3g sat fat, 3g total sugars, 0.8g salt

This impressive dish from the coastal regions of northern Italy is a real treat for lovers of seafood.

INGREDIENTS

1 pound shrimp

2 tablespoons butter

2 shallots, finely chopped

1 cup dry white vermouth

1½ cups water

1 pound dried linguine

2 tablespoons olive oil

1 pound prepared scallops, thawed if frozen

2 tablespoons snipped fresh chives

salt and pepper

1. Peel and devein the shrimp, reserving the shells. Melt the butter in a heavy skillet. Add the shallots and cook over low heat, stirring occasionally, for 5 minutes, or until softened. Add the shrimp shells and cook, stirring continuously, for 1 minute. Pour in the vermouth and cook, stirring, for 1 minute. Add the water, bring to a boil, then reduce the heat and simmer for 10 minutes, or until the liquid has reduced by half. Remove the skillet from the heat.

2. Bring a large saucepan of lightly salted water to a boil. Add the pasta, bring back to a boil, and cook for 8–10 minutes, or according to the package directions, until tender but still firm to the bite.

3. Meanwhile, heat the oil in a separate heavy skillet. Add the scallops and shrimp and cook, stirring frequently, for 2 minutes, or until the scallops are opaque and the shrimp have changed color. Strain the shrimp-shell stock into the skillet. Drain the pasta and add to the skillet with the chives. Season with salt and pepper. Toss well over low heat for 1 minute, then serve.

1

1

3

GOES WELL WITH
Serve with lightly steamed seabean, a type of seaweed, gently tossed with a little melted butter.

Fusilli with Cajun Seafood Sauce

 SERVES 4   PREP TIME: 15 minutes   COOKING TIME: 25 minutes

nutritional information per serving	1,095 cal, 64g fat, 36g sat fat, 7g total sugars, 2.1g salt

If you love hot spices and rich mixtures of cream and cheese, then this is the dish for you.

INGREDIENTS

2 cups heavy whipping cream

8 scallions, thinly sliced

1 cup chopped fresh flat-leaf parsley

1 tablespoon chopped fresh thyme

½ tablespoon pepper

½–1 teaspoon crushed red pepper

1 teaspoon salt

1 pound dried fusilli

½ cup freshly grated Gruyère cheese

¼ cup freshly grated Parmesan cheese

2 tablespoons olive oil

8 ounces shrimp, peeled and deveined

8 ounces scallops, sliced

1 tablespoon shredded fresh basil, to garnish

1. Heat the cream in a large saucepan over medium heat, stirring continuously. When almost boiling, reduce the heat and add the scallions, parsley, thyme, pepper, crushed red pepper, and salt. Simmer for 7–8 minutes, stirring, until thickened. Remove the pan from the heat.

2. Bring a large saucepan of lightly salted water to a boil. Add the pasta, bring back to a boil, and cook for 8–10 minutes, or according to the package directions, until tender but still firm to the bite. Drain and return to the pan. Add the cream mixture and the cheeses to the pasta. Toss over low heat until the cheeses have melted. Transfer to a warm serving dish.

3. Heat the oil in a large skillet over medium–high heat. Add the shrimp and scallops. Cook for 2–3 minutes, until the shrimp have turned opaque and are firm to the touch.

4. Pour the seafood over the pasta and toss to mix. Sprinkle with the basil and serve immediately.

Scallop Soup with Pasta

 SERVES 6

PREP TIME:
15 minutes

COOKING TIME:
25–30 minutes

nutritional information
per serving   444 cal, 15g fat, 8g sat fat, 5g total sugars, 1.6g salt

*If you're planning a formal dinner party, this elegant
soup makes an ideal appetizer.*

INGREDIENTS

1 pound shelled scallops

1½ cups whole milk

6½ cups vegetable stock

1⅔ cups frozen green peas

6 ounces dried tagliolini

5 tablespoons butter

2 scallions, finely chopped

¾ cup dry white wine

3 slices of prosciutto,
cut into thin strips

salt and pepper

chopped fresh flat-leaf parsley,
to garnish

crusty baguette, to serve

1. Slice the scallops in half horizontally and season with salt and pepper.

2. Pour the milk and stock into a saucepan, add a pinch of salt, and bring to a boil. Add the peas and pasta, bring back to a boil, and cook for 8–10 minutes, or according to the package directions, until the pasta is tender but still firm to the bite.

3. Meanwhile, melt the butter in a skillet. Add the scallions and cook over low heat, stirring occasionally, for 3 minutes. Add the scallops and cook for 45 seconds on each side. Pour in the wine, add the prosciutto, and cook for 2–3 minutes.

4. Stir the scallop mixture into the soup, taste, and adjust the seasoning, if necessary, and garnish with the parsley. Serve immediately with the baguette.

GOES WELL WITH
Serve with
bruschetta-thick
slices of lightly
toasted rustic
bread or baguette,
rubbed with
garlic and
drizzled with
olive oil.

Linguine with Clams in Tomato Sauce

 SERVES 4

PREP TIME:
20 minutes

COOKING TIME:
35 minutes

nutritional information per serving	522 cal, 11.5g fat, 2g sat fat, 9g total sugars, 0.7g salt

This Neapolitan speciality features three of the city's favorite ingredients—pasta, tomatoes, and clams.

INGREDIENTS

2¼ pounds live clams, scrubbed

1 cup dry white wine

2 garlic cloves, coarsely chopped

¼ cup chopped fresh flat-leaf parsley

2 tablespoons olive oil

1 onion, chopped

8 plum tomatoes, peeled, seeded, and chopped

1 fresh red chile, seeded and chopped

12 ounces dried linguine

salt and pepper

1. Discard any clams with broken shells or any that refuse to close when tapped. Pour the wine into a large, heavy saucepan and add the garlic, half the parsley, and the clams. Cover and cook over high heat, shaking the pan occasionally, for 5 minutes, or until the shells have opened. Remove the clams with a slotted spoon, reserving the cooking liquid. Discard any that remain closed and remove half of the remainder from their shells. Keep the shelled and unshelled clams in separate covered bowls. Strain the cooking liquid through a cheesecloth-lined strainer and reserve.

2. Heat the oil in a heavy saucepan. Add the onion and cook over low heat for 5 minutes, or until softened. Add the tomatoes, chile, and reserved cooking liquid and season with salt and pepper. Bring to a boil, partly cover the pan, and simmer for 20 minutes.

3. Meanwhile, bring a large saucepan of lightly salted water to a boil. Add the pasta, bring back to a boil, and cook for 8–10 minutes, or according to the package directions, until tender but still firm to the bite. Drain and transfer to a warm serving dish.

4. Stir the shelled clams into the tomato sauce and heat through gently for 2–3 minutes. Pour over the pasta and toss. Garnish with the clams in their shells and remaining parsley. Serve immediately.

Penne with Squid & Tomatoes

SERVES 4   PREP TIME: 15 minutes   COOKING TIME: 30–35 minutes

nutritional information per serving	493 cal, 19g fat, 3g sat fat, 8g total sugars, 0.6g salt

Ask your fish dealer for prepared squid to make this rich southern Italian dish quick and easy to make.

INGREDIENTS

8 ounces dried penne

12 ounces prepared squid

⅓ cup olive oil

2 onions, sliced

1 cup fish or chicken stock

⅔ cup full-bodied red wine

1 (14½-ounce) can diced tomatoes

2 tablespoons tomato paste

1 tablespoon chopped fresh marjoram

1 bay leaf

salt and pepper

2 tablespoons chopped fresh parsley, to garnish

1. Bring a large saucepan of lightly salted water to a boil. Add the pasta, bring back to a boil, and cook for 3 minutes, then drain and reserve until required. With a sharp knife, cut the squid into strips.

2. Heat the oil in a large saucepan. Add the onions and cook over low heat, stirring occasionally, for 5 minutes, or until softened. Add the squid and stock, bring to a boil, and simmer for 3 minutes. Stir in the wine, tomatoes and their can juices, tomato paste, marjoram, and bay leaf. Season with salt and pepper. Bring to a boil and cook for 5 minutes, or until slightly reduced.

3. Add the pasta, return to a boil, and simmer for 5–7 minutes, or according to the package directions, until the pasta is tender but still firm to the bite. Remove and discard the bay leaf. Transfer to a warm serving dish, garnish with the parsley, and serve immediately.

GOES WELL WITH
A simple salad of mixed greens and fresh herbs would be a refreshing accompaniment to this rich and substantial dish.

Mussel & Pasta Soup

 SERVES 4

PREP TIME:
15 minutes

COOKING TIME:
35 minutes

nutritional information per serving	996 cal, 75g fat, 41g sat fat, 4g total sugars, 1.3g salt

This rich and filling soup is full of flavor and would make a great weekend lunch with some crusty bread.

INGREDIENTS

1½ pounds mussels, scrubbed and debearded

2 tablespoons olive oil

1 stick butter

2 ounces bacon, chopped

1 onion, chopped

2 garlic cloves, finely chopped

⅓ cup all-purpose flour

3 Yukon gold or white round potatoes, thinly sliced

4 ounces dried farfalle

1¼ cups heavy cream

1 tablespoon lemon juice

2 egg yolks

salt and pepper

2 tablespoons finely chopped fresh parsley, to garnish

1. Discard any mussels with broken shells or any that refuse to close when tapped. Bring a large, heavy saucepan of water to a boil. Add the mussels and oil and season with pepper. Cover tightly and cook over high heat for 5 minutes, or until the mussels have opened. Remove the mussels with a slotted spoon, discarding any that remain closed. Strain the cooking liquid through a cheesecloth-lined strainer and reserve 5 cups.

2. Melt the butter in a saucepan. Add the bacon, onion, and garlic and cook over low heat, stirring occasionally, for 5 minutes. Stir in the flour and cook, stirring, for 1 minute. Gradually stir in all but 2 tablespoons of the reserved cooking liquid and bring to a boil, stirring continuously. Add the potato slices and simmer for 5 minutes. Add the pasta and simmer for an additional 10 minutes.

3. Stir in the cream and lemon juice and season with salt and pepper. Add the mussels. Mix together the egg yolks and the remaining mussel cooking liquid, then stir the mixture into the soup and cook for 4 minutes, until thickened.

4. Ladle the soup into warm bowls, garnish with chopped parsley, and serve immediately.

Conchiglie with Mussels

 SERVES 6

PREP TIME:
15–20 minutes

COOKING TIME:
25–30 minutes

nutritional information per serving	724 cal, 45g fat, 27g sat fat, 5g total sugars, 0.9g salt

Mussels and pasta make a terrific combination and are popular in all coastal regions of Italy.

INGREDIENTS

2¾ pounds mussels, scrubbed and debearded

1 cup dry white wine

2 large onions, chopped

1 stick unsalted butter

6 large garlic cloves, finely chopped

⅓ cup chopped fresh parsley

1¼ cups heavy cream

1 pound dried conchiglie

salt and pepper

1. Discard any mussels with broken shells or any that refuse to close when tapped. Place the mussels in a large, heavy saucepan, together with the wine and half of the onions. Cover and cook over medium heat, shaking the saucepan frequently, for 2–3 minutes, or until the shells open. Remove the saucepan from the heat. Drain the mussels and reserve the cooking liquid. Discard any mussels that remain closed. Strain the cooking liquid through a cheesecloth-lined strainer into a bowl and reserve.

2. Melt the butter in a saucepan. Add the remaining onions and cook until translucent. Stir in the garlic and cook for 1 minute. Gradually stir in the reserved cooking liquid. Stir in the parsley and cream and season with salt and pepper. Bring to simmering point over low heat.

3. Meanwhile, bring a large saucepan of lightly salted water to a boil. Add the pasta, bring back to a boil, and cook for 8–10 minutes, or according to the package directions, until tender but still firm to the bite. Drain and keep warm.

4. Reserve a few mussels for the garnish and remove the remainder from their shells. Stir the shelled mussels into the cream sauce and warm briefly. Transfer the pasta to a warm dish. Pour the sauce over the pasta and toss. Garnish with the reserved mussels and serve immediately.

Ravioli with Crabmeat & Ricotta

 SERVES 4   PREP TIME: 25 minutes plus resting   COOKING TIME: 10 minutes

nutritional information per serving	570 cal, 28g fat, 14g sat fat, 2g total sugars, 2.2g salt

Homemade ravioli are a special treat and these would make a great impression served at a dinner party.

INGREDIENTS

2⅓ cups type 00 Italian pasta flour or all-purpose flour
1 teaspoon salt
3 eggs, beaten
5 tablespoons butter, melted

filling
1 (6-ounce) can white crabmeat
¾ cup ricotta cheese
finely grated rind of 1 lemon
pinch of crushed red pepper
2 tablespoons chopped fresh flat-leaf parsley
salt and pepper

1. Sift the flour and salt onto a board or work surface, make a well in the center, and add the eggs. Stir with a fork to gradually incorporate the flour into the liquid to form a dough. Knead for about 5 minutes, until the dough is smooth. Wrap in plastic wrap and let rest for 20 minutes.

2. For the filling, stir together the crabmeat, ricotta, lemon rind, crushed red pepper, and parsley. Season with salt and pepper.

3. Roll the dough with a pasta machine or by hand to a thickness of about ⅛ inch and cut into thirty-two 2½-inch squares.

4. Place a spoonful of the filling in the center of half the squares. Brush the edges with water and place the remaining squares on top, pressing to seal.

5. Bring a saucepan of lightly salted water to a boil. Add the ravioli, bring back to a boil, and cook for about 3 minutes, until tender but still firm to the bite. Drain well. Drizzle the melted butter over the ravioli, sprinkle with pepper, and serve immediately.

Farfallini Buttered Lobster

 SERVES 4

PREP TIME:
30–35 minutes

COOKING TIME:
30–35 minutes

nutritional information per serving	764 cal, 34g fat, 20g sat fat, 3g total sugars, 1.6g salt

Wonderfully luxurious, this has to be the ultimate pasta dish for a very special occasion.

INGREDIENTS

2 lobsters, about 1½ pounds each, split into halves

juice and grated rind of 1 lemon

1 stick butter

¼ cup fresh white bread crumbs

2 tablespoons brandy

⅓ cup heavy cream or crème fraîche

1 pound dried farfallini (tiny pasta bow ties)

⅔ cup freshly grated Parmesan cheese

salt and pepper

lemon wedges and fresh dill sprigs, to garnish

1. Preheat the oven to 325°F. Discard the stomach sac, vein, and gills from each lobster. Remove the meat from the tail and chop. Crack the claws and legs, remove the meat, and chop. Transfer the meat to a bowl and add the lemon juice and lemon rind. Clean the shells and place in the oven to dry out.

2. Melt 2 tablespoons of the butter in a skillet. Add the bread crumbs and cook for 3 minutes, until crisp and golden brown. Melt the remaining butter in a separate saucepan. Add the lobster meat and heat through gently. Add the brandy and cook for an additional 3 minutes, then add the cream and season with salt and pepper.

3. Meanwhile, bring a large saucepan of lightly salted water to a boil. Add the pasta, bring back to a boil, and cook for 8–10 minutes, or according to the package directions, until tender but still firm to the bite. Drain and spoon the pasta into the clean lobster shells.

4. Preheat the broiler to medium. Spoon the buttered lobster on top of the pasta and sprinkle with a little Parmesan cheese and the bread crumbs. Broil for 2–3 minutes, or until golden brown. Transfer the lobster shells to a warm plate, garnish with the lemon wedges and dill sprigs, and serve immediately.

Fresh Tomato Soup with Pasta *168*

Hearty Bean & Pasta Soup *170*

Potato & Pasta Soup with Pesto *172*

Tomato, Olive & Mozzarella Pasta Salad *174*

Chile Broccoli Pasta *176*

Macaroni & Double Cheese *178*

Penne with Asparagus & Blue Cheese *180*

Rigatoni with Red Pepper & Goat cheese *182*

Pasta with Camembert *184*

Creamy Asparagus & Brie Tagliatelle *186*

Linguine with Lemon, Chile & Spinach *188*

Spaghetti Olio E Aglio *190*

Pasta with Leek & Butternut Squash *192*

Conchiglie with Marinated Artichoke *194*

Spicy Eggplant, Chickpea & Cilantro Penne *196*

Ziti with Arugula *198*

Garlic Mushroom Pasta *200*

Linguine with Wild Mushrooms *202*

Macaroni with Chickpeas, Herbs & Garlic *204*

Pappardelle with Cherry Tomatoes, Arugula & Mozzarella *206*

Pasta with Roasted Vegetables & Toasted Almonds *208*

Creamy Ricotta, Mint & Garlic Pasta *210*

Creamy Pea & Watercress Pasta *212*

Fusilli with Zucchini & Lemon *214*

Vegetarian

Fresh Tomato Soup
with Pasta

 SERVES 4

PREP TIME:
15 minutes

COOKING TIME:
1 hour

nutritional information
per serving
135 cal, 3.5g fat, 0.6g sat fat, 6g total sugars, 0.4g salt

Tomatoes are our major source of dietary lycopene, a carotene antioxidant that fights heart disease and may help prevent prostate cancer. They also contain vitamin C, quercetin, and lutein.

INGREDIENTS

1 tablespoon olive oil
4 large plum tomatoes
1 onion, cut into quarters
1 garlic clove, thinly sliced
1 celery stalk, coarsely chopped
2 cups vegetable stock
2 ounces dried soup pasta
salt and pepper
chopped fresh flat-leaf parsley,
to garnish

1. Pour the oil into a large, heavy saucepan and add the tomatoes, onion, garlic, and celery. Cover and cook over low heat, occasionally shaking gently, for 45 minutes, until pulpy.

2. Transfer the mixture to a food processor or blender and process to a smooth puree.

3. Push the puree through a strainer into a clean saucepan.

4. Add the stock and bring to a boil. Add the pasta, bring back to a boil, and cook for 8–10 minutes, or according to the package directions, until the pasta is tender but still firm to the bite. Season with salt and pepper. Ladle into warm bowls, garnish with parsley, and serve immediately.

1

3

4

VARIATION:
Replace the chopped
fresh parsley with
the same amount of
chopped fresh chives
and serve with
freshly grated
Parmesan cheese
sprinkled on the top.

Hearty Bean & Pasta Soup

 SERVES 4   PREP TIME: 10 minutes   COOKING TIME: 40 minutes

nutritional information per serving	456 cal, 16g fat, 4g sat fat, 8g total sugars, 1.3g salt

Add a little Tuscan sunshine to your dinner table with this colorful and satisfying traditional soup.

INGREDIENTS

¼ cup olive oil

1 onion, finely chopped

1 celery stalk, finely chopped

1 carrot, diced

1 bay leaf

5 cups vegetable stock

1 (14½-ounce) can diced tomatoes

6 ounces dried farfalle

1 (15-ounce) can cannellini beans, drained and rinsed

7 ounces spinach or Swiss chard, thick stems removed and shredded

salt and pepper

½ cup finely grated vegetarian Parmesan-style cheese, to serve

1. Heat the oil in a large, heavy saucepan. Add the onion, celery, and carrot and cook over medium heat for 10 minutes, stirring occasionally, until the vegetables are slightly soft. Add the bay leaf, stock, and tomatoes, then bring to a boil.

2. Reduce the heat, cover, and simmer for 15 minutes, or until the vegetables are just tender. Add the pasta and beans, bring back to a boil, and cook for 8–10 minutes, or according to package directions, until the pasta is tender but still firm to the bite.

3. Stir occasionally to prevent the pasta from sticking to the bottom of the pan and burning. Season with salt and pepper, add the spinach, and cook for an additional 2 minutes, or until tender. Remove and discard the bay leaf. Ladle the soup into warm bowls and serve immediately with grated Parmesan cheese.

Potato & Pasta Soup with Pesto

 SERVES 4   PREP TIME: 15 minutes   COOKING TIME: 45 minutes

nutritional information per serving	985 cal, 73.6g fat, 24.1g sat fat, 15.7g total sugars, 0.9g salt

The simplest of fresh ingredients are combined to make this appetizing meal-in-a-bowl soup.

INGREDIENTS

3 slices pancetta, chopped

2 tablespoons olive oil

4 Yukon gold or white round potatoes, peeled and finely chopped

4 onions, finely chopped

2½ cups vegetable stock

2½ cups whole milk

4 ounces dried conchigliette (small pasta shells)

⅔ cup heavy cream

2 tablespoons chopped fresh flat-leaf parsley

salt and pepper

vegetarian Parmesan-style cheese shavings, to serve

parsley pesto

1 cup fresh flat-leaf parsley leaves

2 garlic cloves, chopped

⅓ cup pine nuts

2 tablespoons chopped fresh basil leaves

⅔ cup vegetarian Parmesan-style cheese, grated

⅔ cup olive oil

1. To make the pesto, put all of the ingredients in a food processor or blender and process for 2 minutes, or blend by hand using a mortar and pestle.

2. Cook the pancetta in a large saucepan over medium heat for 4 minutes. Add the oil, potatoes, and onions and cook, stirring continuously, for 12 minutes.

3. Add the stock and milk to the pan, bring to a boil, and simmer for 10 minutes. Add the pasta, bring back to a boil, and cook for 8–10 minutes, or according to the package directions, until tender but still firm to the bite.

4. Stir in the cream and simmer for 5 minutes. Add the chopped parsley and 2 tablespoons of the pesto. Season with salt and pepper. Ladle the soup into serving bowls and serve immediately with the vegetarian Parmesan-style cheese shavings.

Tomato, Olive & Mozzarella Pasta Salad

 SERVES 4   PREP TIME: 5 minutes   COOKING TIME: 15 minutes

nutritional information per serving	385 cal, 36g fat, 10g sat fat, 8g total sugars, 0.7g salt

When you taste this classic combination of ingredients, you'll know why it is so popular in Italy.

INGREDIENTS

8 ounces dried conchiglie (pasta shells)

⅓ cup pine nuts

2½ cups halved cherry tomatoes

1 red bell pepper, seeded and cut into bite-size chunks

1 red onion, chopped

8 ounces mozzarella di bufala, cut into small pieces

12 ripe black olives, pitted

1 cup fresh basil leaves

vegetarian Parmesan-style cheese shavings, to garnish

salt

dressing

⅓ cup extra virgin olive oil

2 tablespoons balsamic vinegar

1 tablespoon chopped fresh basil

salt and pepper

1. Bring a large saucepan of lightly salted water to a boil. Add the pasta, bring back to a boil, and cook for 8–10 minutes, or according to the package directions, until tender but still firm to the bite. Drain thoroughly and let cool.

2. Meanwhile, heat a dry skillet over low heat, add the pine nuts, and cook, shaking the skillet frequently, for 1–2 minutes, until lightly toasted. Remove from the heat, transfer to a dish, and let cool.

3. To make the dressing, put all the ingredients in a small bowl and mix together well. Cover with plastic wrap and set aside.

4. Divide the pasta among four serving bowls. Add the pine nuts, tomatoes, bell pepper, onion, mozzarella, and olives to each bowl. Sprinkle with the basil, then drizzle with the dressing. Garnish with vegetarian Parmesan-style cheese shavings and serve.

Chile Broccoli Pasta

 SERVES 4

PREP TIME: 5 minutes

COOKING TIME: 10–15 minutes

nutritional information per serving	300 cal, 11g fat, 1.5g sat fat, 3g total sugars, trace salt

A dish made with these ingredients can't fail—they just seem right together. Good for serving to a crowd.

INGREDIENTS

8 ounces dried penne or macaroni

3 cups broccoli florets

¼ cup extra virgin olive oil

2 large garlic cloves, chopped

2 fresh red chiles, seeded and diced

8 cherry tomatoes

handful of fresh basil leaves, to garnish

salt

1. Bring a large saucepan of lightly salted water to a boil. Add the pasta, return to a boil, and cook according to the package directions, until tender but still firm to the bite. Drain the pasta, refresh under cold running water, and drain again. Set aside.

2. Bring a separate saucepan of lightly salted water to a boil, add the broccoli, and cook for 5 minutes. Drain, refresh under cold running water, and drain again.

3. Heat the oil in a large, heavy skillet over high heat. Add the garlic, chiles, and tomatoes and cook, stirring continuously, for 1 minute.

4. Add the broccoli and mix well. Cook for 2 minutes, stirring, to heat all the way through. Add the pasta and mix well again. Cook for an additional minute. Transfer the pasta to a large, warm serving bowl and serve immediately, garnished with basil leaves.

1

3

4

COOK'S NOTE

Don't be tempted to chop fresh basil with a knife—it will turn black. Use small leaves or tear larger ones into pieces.

Macaroni & Double Cheese

🍽️ SERVES 4   👨‍🍳 PREP TIME: 10 minutes   ⏱️ COOKING TIME: 15 minutes

nutritional information per serving	1,109 cal, 66g fat, 24g sat fat, 9g total sugars, 3g salt

This is an especially rich and tasty variation of a family favorite, equally popular with children and adults.

INGREDIENTS

8 ounces dried macaroni

1 cup ricotta cheese

1½ tablespoons whole-grain mustard

3 tablespoons snipped fresh chives, plus extra to garnish

12 cherry tomatoes, halved

⅔ cup drained and chopped sun-dried tomatoes in oil

butter or oil, for greasing

1 cup shredded cheddar cheese,

salt and pepper

1. Preheat the broiler to high. Bring a large saucepan of lightly salted water to a boil. Add the pasta, bring back to a boil, and cook for 8–10 minutes, or according to the package directions, until tender but still firm to the bite. Drain.

2. In a large bowl, mix the ricotta with the mustard and chives and season with salt and pepper.

3. Stir in the macaroni, cherry tomatoes, and sun-dried tomatoes and mix well.

4. Grease a 2-quart shallow ovenproof dish. Spoon in the macaroni mixture, spreading evenly.

5. Sprinkle the cheddar cheese over the macaroni mixture and cook under the preheated broiler for 4–5 minutes, until golden and bubbling. Serve the macaroni immediately, sprinkled with extra chives.

2

3

4

COOK'S NOTE
For an even
richer dish,
tear 4 ounces
mozzarella into
small pieces
and stir into the
macaroni with
the tomatoes.

Penne with Asparagus & Blue Cheese

 SERVES 4   PREP TIME: 10 minutes   COOKING TIME: 25 minutes

nutritional information per serving	805 cal, 48g fat, 28g sat fat, 5g total sugars, 1.1g salt

It's hard to believe that a dish so stunning is also so simple and requires almost no effort to prepare.

INGREDIENTS

1 pound asparagus spears

1 tablespoon olive oil

8 ounces vegetarian blue cheese, crumbled

¾ cup heavy cream

12 ounces dried penne

salt and pepper

1. Preheat the oven to 450°F. Place the asparagus spears in a single layer in a shallow ovenproof dish. Sprinkle with the oil and season with salt and pepper. Turn to coat in the oil and seasoning. Roast in the preheated oven for 10–12 minutes, until slightly browned and just tender. Set aside and keep warm.

2. Combine the cheese with the cream in a bowl. Season with salt and pepper.

3. Bring a large saucepan of lightly salted water to a boil. Add the pasta, bring back to a boil, and cook for 8–10 minutes, or according to the package directions, until tender but still firm to the bite. Drain and transfer to a warm serving dish. Immediately add the asparagus and the cheese mixture. Toss well until the cheese has melted and the pasta is coated with the sauce. Serve immediately.

1    2    3

GOES WELL WITH
Freshly baked sourdough bread would be just the thing for mopping up every last bit of this delicious creamy sauce.

Rigatoni with Red Pepper & Goat Cheese

SERVES 4

PREP TIME:
15 minutes

COOKING TIME:
35 minutes

nutritional information
per serving | 637 cal, 21g fat, 9g sat fat, 13g total sugars, 0.7g salt

Tangy cheese, slightly sharp red peppers, and succulent olives are combined in a rich and pungent sauce.

INGREDIENTS

2 tablespoons olive oil

1 tablespoon butter

1 small onion, finely chopped

4 red bell peppers, seeded and
cut into ¾-inch squares

3 garlic cloves, thinly sliced

1 pound dried rigatoni

4 ounces goat cheese, crumbled

15 fresh basil leaves, shredded

10 ripe black olives,
pitted and sliced

salt and pepper

1. Heat the oil and butter in a large skillet over medium heat. Add the onion, and cook until soft. Increase the heat to medium–high and add the bell peppers and garlic. Cook for 12–15 minutes, stirring, until the bell peppers are tender but not mushy. Season with salt and pepper. Remove from the heat.

2. Bring a large saucepan of lightly salted water to a boil. Add the pasta, bring back to a boil, and cook for 8–10 minutes, or until tender but still firm to the bite. Drain and transfer to a warm serving dish. Add the goat cheese and toss to mix.

3. Briefly reheat the sauce. Add the basil and olives. Pour the sauce over the pasta and toss well to mix. Serve immediately.

GOES WELL WITH
A salad of peppery
greens, such as arugula
and radicchio, makes
a delicious contrast to
serve with this dish.

Pasta with Camembert

 SERVES 4

PREP TIME:
5 minutes

COOKING TIME:
20 minutes

nutritional information per serving	722 cal, 46g fat, 28g sat fat, 2g total sugars, 0.9g salt

This rich and creamy dish looks especially appetizing if you use green pasta to contrast the light sauce.

INGREDIENTS

4 tablespoons unsalted butter

8 ounces Camembert cheese, rind removed, diced

⅔ cup heavy cream

2 tablespoons dry white wine

1 teaspoon cornstarch

1 tablespoon chopped chervil

10 ounces dried tagliatelle or fettuccine

salt and pepper

green salad, to serve

1. Melt half the butter in a heavy saucepan. Add three-quarters of the cheese and cook over low heat for about 2 minutes, until melted.

2. Beat in the cream, wine, and cornstarch and stir in the chervil. Cook, beating continuously, until thickened and smooth, then remove from the heat.

3. Bring a large saucepan of lightly salted water to a boil. Add the pasta, bring back to a boil, and cook for 8–10 minutes, or according to the package directions, until tender but still firm to the bite. Drain, return to the pan, and toss with the remaining butter.

4. Return the pan of cheese sauce to low heat and reheat gently, beating continuously. Divide the pasta among warm plates. Spoon the cheese sauce over it, sprinkle with the remaining cheese, and serve immediately with a green salad.

SOMETHING DIFFERENT

For a sauce with a more powerful, but still subtle flavor, use a blue cheese, such as Gorgonzola.

Linguine with Lemon, Chile & Spinach

SERVES 4

PREP TIME:
10 minutes

COOKING TIME:
25 minutes

nutritional information
per serving
540 cal, 21g fat, 8g sat fat, 4g total sugars, 0.7g salt

*The wonderful, light, summery flavors make this a
perfect dish for an alfresco meal and
it's great for easy entertaining.*

INGREDIENTS

12 ounces dried linguine

2 tablespoons olive oil, plus extra
for drizzling

2 garlic cloves, finely chopped

1 red chile, seeded and
finely chopped

finely grated rind and juice
of 1 lemon

8 ounces ricotta cheese

1 (12-ounce) package
baby spinach,

¼ cup freshly grated vegetarian
Parmesan-style cheese

salt and pepper

1. Bring a large saucepan of lightly salted water to a boil. Add the pasta, bring back to a boil, and cook for 8–10 minutes, or according to the package directions, until tender but still firm to the bite. Drain, reserving ⅓ cup of the cooking liquid, then return to the pan. Drizzle with a little oil, toss gently, and set aside.

2. Heat the oil in another saucepan, add the garlic and chile, and cook over low heat, stirring frequently, for 2 minutes. Stir in the lemon rind and juice, ricotta cheese, and reserved cooking liquid. Season with salt and pepper and bring to simmering point, stirring frequently.

3. Add the spinach, in 2–3 batches, and cook for 2–3 minutes, until wilted. Taste and adjust the seasoning, if necessary, then transfer the sauce to the pan of pasta. Toss well, then divide among warm plates. Sprinkle with the vegetarian Parmesan-style cheese and serve immediately.

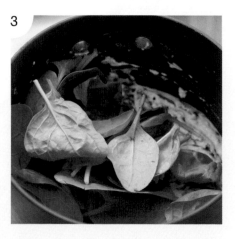

COOK'S NOTE

If you warm the lemon on high in the microwave for a few seconds, it will yield more juice when you squeeze it.

Spaghetti Olio E Aglio

SERVES 4

PREP TIME: 5 minutes

COOKING TIME: 15 minutes

nutritional information per serving	590 cal, 25g fat, 3.5g sat fat, 3.5g total sugars, trace salt

An inexpensive dish created by the poor, this classic from Rome is now popular throughout Italy.

INGREDIENTS

1 pound dried spaghetti

½ cup extra virgin olive oil

3 garlic cloves, finely chopped

3 tablespoons chopped fresh flat-leaf parsley

salt and pepper

1. Bring a large saucepan of lightly salted water to a boil. Add the pasta, bring back to a boil, and cook for 8–10 minutes, or according to the package directions, until tender but still firm to the bite.

2. Meanwhile, heat the oil in a heavy skillet. Add the garlic and a pinch of salt and cook over low heat, stirring continuously, for 3–4 minutes, or until golden. Do not let the garlic brown or it will taste bitter. Remove the skillet from the heat.

3. Drain the pasta and transfer to a warm serving dish. Pour in the garlic-flavored oil, then add the chopped parsley and season with salt and pepper. Toss well and serve immediately.

TO SERVE
Cooked pasta gets cold quickly, so make sure to transfer to a warm serving plate once drained.

Pasta with Leek & Butternut Squash

 SERVES 4   PREP TIME: 15 minutes   COOKING TIME: 40 minutes

nutritional information per serving	334 cal, 5g fat, 1.5g sat fat, 9g total sugars, 0.4g salt

This unusual dish combines the sweetness of roasted vegetables with warm spice and aromatic cilantro.

INGREDIENTS

2 cups ¾-inch baby leeks slices

1½ cups butternut squash chunks

1½ tablespoons medium curry paste

1 teaspoon vegetable oil

10 cherry tomatoes

8 ounces dried farfalle

2 tablespoons chopped fresh cilantro

salt

white sauce

1 cup skim milk

3 tablespoons cornstarch

1 teaspoon dry mustard

1 small onion, left whole

2 small bay leaves

4 teaspoons grated vegetarian Parmesan-style cheese

1. To make the white sauce, put the milk into a saucepan with the cornstarch, dry mustard, onion, and bay leaves. Beat over medium heat until thick. Remove from the heat, discard the onion and bay leaves, and stir in the cheese. Set aside, stirring occasionally to prevent a skin from forming. Preheat the oven to 400°F.

2. Bring a large saucepan of water to a boil, add the leeks, and cook for 2 minutes. Add the butternut squash and cook for an additional 2 minutes. Drain in a colander. Mix the curry paste with the oil in a large bowl. Toss the leeks and butternut squash in the mixture to coat thoroughly.

3. Transfer the leeks and squash to a nonstick baking sheet and roast in the preheated oven for 10 minutes, until golden brown. Add the tomatoes and roast for an additional 5 minutes.

4. Meanwhile, bring a large saucepan of lightly salted water to a boil. Add the pasta, bring back to a boil, and cook for 8–10 minutes, or according to the package directions, until tender but still firm to the bite. Drain well. Put the white sauce into a large saucepan and warm over low heat. Add the leeks, squash, tomatoes, and cilantro and stir in the pasta. Transfer to warm plates and serve immediately.

Conchiglie with Marinated Artichoke

 SERVES 4

PREP TIME:
10 minutes

COOKING TIME:
50 minutes

nutritional information per serving	500 cal, 19g fat, 3.5g sat fat, 7g total sugars, 1.4g salt

This would be an excellent choice for an unusual first course for a formal dinner party.

INGREDIENTS

3 tablespoons olive oil

1 onion, finely chopped

3 garlic cloves, crushed

1 teaspoon dried oregano

½ teaspoon crushed red pepper

12 marinated artichoke hearts from a can, drained and marinade reserved

1 (14½-ounce) can diced tomatoes

12 ounces dried conchiglie (pasta shells)

4 teaspoons freshly grated vegetarian Parmesan-style cheese

3 tablespoons chopped fresh flat-leaf parsley

salt and pepper

1. Heat the oil in a large, deep skillet over medium heat. Add the onion and sauté for 5 minutes, until translucent. Add the garlic, oregano, crushed red pepper, and the reserved artichoke marinade. Cook for an additional 5 minutes.

2. Stir in the tomatoes. Bring to a boil, then simmer over medium-low heat for 30 minutes. Season with salt and pepper.

3. Bring a large saucepan of lightly salted water to a boil. Add the pasta, bring back to a boil, and cook for 8–10 minutes, or according to the package directions, until tender but still firm to the bite. Drain and transfer to a warm serving dish.

4. Cut the artichokes into quarters and add to the sauce with the vegetarian Parmesan-style cheese and parsley. Cook for a few minutes, until heated through. Pour the sauce over the pasta, toss well to mix, and serve immediately.

Spicy Eggplant, Chickpea & Cilantro Penne

 SERVES 4   PREP TIME: 15 minutes   COOKING TIME: 45 minutes

nutritional information per serving	444 cal, 9g fat, 1g sat fat, 10g total sugars, 0.8g salt

Pasta with more than a hint of North African cuisine makes a wonderfully warming and unusual dish.

INGREDIENTS

large pinch of saffron threads

2 cups hot vegetable stock

2 tablespoons olive oil

1 large onion, coarsely chopped

1 teaspoon cumin seeds, crushed

4 cups diced eggplant

1 large red bell pepper, seeded and chopped

1 (14½-ounce) can diced tomatoes with garlic

1 teaspoon ground cinnamon

¾ cup fresh cilantro, leaves and stems separated and coarsely chopped

1 (15-ounce) can chickpeas, drained and rinsed

10 ounces dried penne

salt and pepper

harissa or chili sauce, to serve (optional)

1. Toast the saffron threads in a dry skillet set over medium heat for 20–30 seconds, just until they begin to give off their aroma. Place in a small bowl and crumble with your fingers. Add 2 tablespoons of the hot stock and set aside to steep.

2. Heat the oil in a large saucepan. Add the onion and sauté for 5–6 minutes, until golden brown. Add the cumin seeds and cook for an additional 20-30 seconds.

3. Stir in the eggplant, red bell pepper, tomatoes, cinnamon, coriander stems, saffron liquid, and remaining stock. Cover and simmer for 20 minutes.

4. Add the chickpeas to the pan and season with salt and pepper. Simmer for an additional 5 minutes, removing the lid to reduce and thicken the sauce, if necessary.

5. Bring a large saucepan of lightly salted water to a boil. Add the pasta, bring back to a boil, and cook for 8–10 minutes, or according to the package directions, until tender but still firm to the bite. Drain and transfer to a warm serving bowl. Add the sauce and half the cilantro leaves, then toss. Garnish with the remaining cilantro and serve immediately with harissa or chili sauce, if desired.

Garlic Mushroom Pasta

SERVES 4

PREP TIME:
15 minutes

COOKING TIME:
25 minutes

nutritional information
per serving

804 cal, 51g fat, 25g sat fat, 4g total sugars, 0.6g salt

The perfect choice for a midweek dinner, this speedy dish is full of flavor but requires very little effort to prepare.

INGREDIENTS

1 pound dried spaghetti

¼ cup olive oil

1½ pounds oyster mushrooms, torn into large pieces

3 garlic cloves, finely chopped

4 tablespoons butter

1 teaspoon chopped fresh thyme

1 tablespoon chopped fresh flat-leaf parsley

1 cup heavy cream

salt and pepper

grated Parmesan-style vegetarian cheese, to serve

1. Bring a large saucepan of lightly salted water to a boil. Add the pasta, bring back to a boil, and cook for 8–10 minutes, or according to the package directions, until tender but still firm to the bite.

2. Meanwhile, heat the oil in a large skillet, add the mushrooms, and cook over high heat, stirring occasionally, for 3–4 minutes, until lightly browned. Reduce the heat, add the garlic, and cook, stirring occasionally, for an additional 6–8 minutes.

3. Drain the pasta and return it to the pan. Add the butter, season with pepper, and toss well.

4. Stir the thyme and parsley into the pan of mushrooms, season with salt and pepper, and stir in the cream. Remove the pan from the heat. Transfer the pasta to a warm serving dish, top with the mushroom mixture, and serve immediately, with the cheese separately.

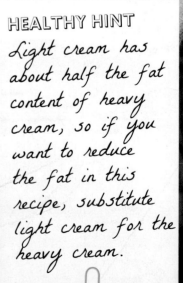

HEALTHY HINT
Light cream has about half the fat content of heavy cream, so if you want to reduce the fat in this recipe, substitute light cream for the heavy cream.

Macaroni with Chickpeas, Herbs & Garlic

SERVES 4

PREP TIME:
5 minutes

COOKING TIME:
20 minutes

nutritional information
per serving   464 cal, 12g fat, 1.5g sat fat, 3.5g total sugars, 0.4g salt

A filling and warming dish, this will satisfy even the heartiest appetite on a chilly winter evening.

INGREDIENTS

12 ounces dried macaroni

3 tablespoons olive oil

1 onion, finely chopped

1 garlic clove, crushed

1 (15-ounce) can chickpeas, drained

¼ cup tomato puree

2 tablespoons chopped fresh oregano

small handful of basil leaves, shredded, plus extra sprigs to garnish

salt and pepper

1. Bring a large saucepan of lightly salted water to a boil. Add the pasta, bring back to a boil, and cook for 8–10 minutes, or according to the package directions, until tender but still firm to the bite. Drain thoroughly.

2. Meanwhile, heat the oil in a saucepan and sauté the onion and garlic, stirring occasionally, for 4–5 minutes, until golden.

3. Add the chickpeas and tomato puree to the pan and stir until heated through.

4. Stir the pasta into the pan with the oregano and shredded basil. Season with salt and pepper and serve immediately.

GOES WELL WITH
The slightly chewy texture and distinct aroma of rosemary or onion focaccia would be just right with this dish.

Pasta with Roasted Vegetables & Toasted Almonds

SERVES 4   PREP TIME: 20 minutes   COOKING TIME: 1 hour

nutritional information per serving	542 cal, 23g fat, 3g sat fat, 10g total sugars, trace salt

With its attractive appearance and appetizing aroma, this colorful dish is guaranteed to become a family favorite.

INGREDIENTS

1 eggplant, coarsely diced

1 red bell pepper, seeded and diced

1 yellow bell pepper, seeded and diced

2 zucchini, coarsely diced

⅓ cup olive oil

2 tablespoons chopped fresh parsley

12 cherry tomatoes, halved

2 garlic cloves, finely chopped

12 ounces dried rigatoni

¼ cup slivered almonds

salt and pepper

1. Preheat the oven to 350°F. Put the eggplant, red bell pepper, yellow bell pepper, and zucchini into a roasting pan. Drizzle with half the oil, sprinkle with the parsley, and season with salt and pepper. Roast in the preheated oven for 30 minutes. Remove the pan from the oven, add the tomatoes and garlic, toss well, and return to the oven. Roast for an additional 30 minutes.

2. Shortly before the vegetables are ready, bring a large saucepan of lightly salted water to a boil. Add the pasta, bring back to a boil, and cook for 8–10 minutes, or according to the package directions, until tender but still firm to the bite.

3. Meanwhile, heat 1 tablespoon of the remaining oil in a small skillet, add the almonds, and cook over low heat, shaking the skillet often, for 2–3 minutes, until the almonds are golden. Drain on paper towels.

4. Drain the pasta and transfer to a warm serving dish. Add the roasted vegetables, drizzle with the remaining oil, and toss. Garnish with the toasted almonds and serve immediately.

SOMETHING DIFFERENT

This dish is also excellent served cold. Let the pasta and vegetables cool before garnishing with the almonds.

Creamy Ricotta, Mint & Garlic Pasta

 SERVES 4   PREP TIME: 5 minutes   COOKING TIME: 15 minutes

nutritional information per serving	500 cal, 25g fat, 15g sat fat, 3g total sugars, 0.1g salt

This is a wonderful choice for a summery meal when you want to minimize the time spent in the kitchen.

INGREDIENTS

10 ounces dried fusilli

½ cup ricotta cheese

1–2 roasted garlic cloves from a jar, finely chopped

⅔ cup heavy cream

1 tablespoon chopped fresh mint, plus extra sprigs to garnish

salt and pepper

fresh crusty bread, to serve

1. Bring a large saucepan of lightly salted water to a boil. Add the pasta, bring back to a boil, and cook for 8–10 minutes, or according to the package directions, until tender but still firm to the bite.

2. Beat together the ricotta, garlic, cream, and chopped mint in a bowl until smooth.

3. Drain the pasta, then return it to the pan. Pour in the cheese mixture and toss together.

4. Season with pepper and serve immediately with fresh crusty bread.

GOES WELL WITH
A light cucumber and watermelon salad would be a cooling and refreshing accompaniment to this creamy dish.

Creamy Pea & Watercress Pasta

 SERVES 4

PREP TIME:
20 minutes

COOKING TIME:
30 minutes

nutritional information per serving	434 cal, 6.5g fat, 2g sat fat, 4g total sugars, 0.4g salt

The peppery sharpness of watercress goes beautifully with the sweetness of fresh young peas in this lovely summery dish.

INGREDIENTS

1 tablespoon olive oil

1 garlic clove, finely chopped

2 shallots, finely chopped

2 cups shelled peas

2 tablespoons chopped sage

2 cups vegetable stock

12 ounces dried penne

½ bunch fresh watercress, stems removed, or 5 cups arugula

finely grated rind and juice of 1 lemon

2 tablespoons Greek-style yogurt

salt and white pepper

fresh crusty bread, to serve

1. Heat the oil in a saucepan, add the garlic and shallots, and cook over low heat, stirring occasionally, for 4–5 minutes, until soft. Add the peas, sage, and stock, increase the heat to medium, and bring to a boil. Reduce the heat and simmer for 10–15 minutes, until the peas are tender.

2. Meanwhile, bring a large saucepan of lightly salted water to a boil. Add the pasta, bring back to a boil, and cook for 8–10 minutes, or according to the package directions, until tender but still firm to the bite. Drain and return to the pan.

3. Drain the vegetables, reserving 2 tablespoons of the stock. Put the vegetables, reserved stock, and watercress into a food processor or blender and process briefly to a coarse puree. Scrape the puree into the pan of pasta, add the lemon rind and juice and yogurt, season with salt and pepper, and toss well. Transfer to warm bowls and serve immediately with the fresh crusty bread.

1

1

3

COOK'S NOTE
For extra flavor, add some of the (rinsed) pea pods to the pan when cooking the peas, but remove them before processing.

Fusilli with Zucchini & Lemon

SERVES 4   PREP TIME: 10 minutes   COOKING TIME: 25–30 minutes

nutritional information per serving	629 cal, 23g fat, 6g sat fat, 6g total sugars, 0.3g salt

Deliciously fragrant, this light, summery dish would be a great choice for informal alfresco entertaining.

INGREDIENTS

⅓ cup olive oil

1 small onion, thinly sliced

2 garlic cloves, minced

2 tablespoons chopped fresh rosemary

1 tablespoon chopped fresh flat-leaf parsley

4 small zucchini, cut into 1½-inch strips

finely grated rind of 1 lemon

1 pound dried fusilli

salt and pepper

¼ cup grated vegetarian Parmesan-style cheese, to serve

1. Heat the oil in a large skillet over low–medium heat. Add the onion and cook gently, stirring occasionally, for about 10 minutes, until golden.

2. Increase the heat to medium–high. Add the garlic, rosemary, and parsley. Cook for a few seconds, stirring.

3. Add the zucchini and lemon rind. Cook for 5–7 minutes, stirring occasionally, until just tender. Season with salt and pepper. Remove from the heat.

4. Bring a large saucepan of lightly salted water to a boil. Add the pasta, bring back to a boil, and cook for 8–10 minutes, or according to the package directions, until tender but still firm to the bite.

5. Drain the pasta and transfer to a warm serving dish. Briefly reheat the zucchini sauce. Pour over the pasta and toss well to mix. Serve immediately with the vegetarian Parmesan-style cheese.

2

5

5

GOES WELL WITH
A salad of bean sprouts, grapes, and chopped nuts dressed with a nut oil vinaigrette will provide a delightful crunch factor.

Filled & Baked

Lasagna al Forno

 SERVES 6   PREP TIME: 15 minutes   COOKING TIME: 2¼ hours

nutritional information
per serving   629 cal, 71g fat, 30g sat fat, 5g total sugars, 2.8g salt

You need plenty of time to make a baked lasagna with an authentic flavor, but it is worth it.

INGREDIENTS

¾ cup olive oil

4 tablespoons butter

4 ounces pancetta

1 onion, finely chopped

1 celery stalk, finely chopped

1 carrot, finely chopped

12 ounces chuck steak, in a single piece

⅓ cup red wine

2 tablespoons tomato paste

8 ounces Italian link sausages

2 eggs

1¾ cups freshly grated Parmesan cheese

⅔ cup fresh bread crumbs

1⅓ cups ricotta cheese

8 dried oven-ready lasagna noodles

12 ounces mozzarella cheese, sliced

salt and pepper

chopped fresh parsley, to garnish

1. Heat ½ cup of the oil with the butter in a large saucepan. Add the pancetta, onion, celery, and carrot and cook over low heat, until soft. Increase the heat to medium, add the steak, and cook until evenly browned. Stir in the wine and tomato paste, season with salt and pepper, and bring to a boil. Reduce the heat, cover, and simmer gently for 1½ hours, until the steak is tender.

2. Meanwhile, heat 2 tablespoons of the remaining oil in a skillet. Add the sausage and cook for 8–10 minutes. Remove from the skillet and discard the skin. Thinly slice the sausage and set aside. Transfer the steak to a cutting board and finely dice. Return half the steak to the sauce.

3. Mix the remaining steak in a bowl with 1 egg, 1 tablespoon of the Parmesan cheese, and the bread crumbs. Shape into walnut-size balls. Heat the remaining oil in a skillet, add the meatballs, and cook for 5–8 minutes, until brown. Pass the ricotta through a strainer into a bowl. Stir in the remaining egg and ¼ cup of the remaining Parmesan cheese.

4. Preheat the oven to 350°F. In a rectangular ovenproof dish, make layers with the lasagna noodles, ricotta mixture, meat sauce, meatballs, sausage, and mozzarella cheese. Finish with a layer of the ricotta mixture and sprinkle with the remaining Parmesan cheese.

5. Bake the lasagna in the preheated oven for 20–25 minutes, until golden and bubbling. Serve immediately, garnished with chopped parsley.

Warm Ravioli Salad

 SERVES 4   PREP TIME: 20 minutes   COOKING TIME: 15 minutes

nutritional information per serving	748 cal, 41g fat, 12g sat fat, 12g total sugars, 1.3g salt

This is a great dish for easy entertaining because it looks and tastes wonderful but requires little effort.

INGREDIENTS

½ cup olive oil

2 tablespoons balsamic vinegar

1 teaspoon Dijon mustard

1 teaspoon sugar

½ small cucumber, peeled

1 (8-ounce) package mixed salad greens

1 (5-ounce) package arugula

1 head endive, leaves separated

3 tablespoons mixed chopped herbs, such as parsley, thyme, and cilantro

2 tomatoes, cut into wedges

2 roasted red peppers preserved in oil, drained and sliced

20 fresh beef ravioli

2 tablespoons butter

salt and pepper

1. Beat together all but 2 tablespoons of the oil, the vinegar, mustard, and sugar in a bowl and season with salt and pepper. Set aside.

2. Halve the cucumber lengthwise and scoop out the seeds, then slice. Tear the lettuce and arugula leaves into small pieces. Put the cucumber, lettuce, arugula, endive, herbs, tomatoes, and roasted peppers into a bowl and set aside.

3. Bring a large saucepan of lightly salted water to a boil. Add the ravioli and cook according to the package directions, then drain. Melt the butter with the remaining oil in a skillet. Add the ravioli and cook over medium heat, turning carefully once or twice, for 5 minutes, until golden on both sides. Remove the skillet from the heat.

4. Pour the dressing over the salad and toss, then divide among individual serving plates. Top with the ravioli and serve immediately.

Sicilian Spaghetti Cake

 SERVES 4   PREP TIME: 15 minutes   COOKING TIME: 1¼ hours

nutritional information per serving	772 cal, 51g fat, 17g sat fat, 10.5g total sugars, 1.1g salt

This delicious classic dish is perfect for both a family midweek dinner or a special occasion main meal.

INGREDIENTS

½ cup olive oil, plus extra for greasing

2 eggplants, sliced

12 ounces ground beef

1 onion, chopped

2 garlic cloves, chopped finely

2 tablespoons tomato paste

1 (14½-ounce) can diced tomatoes

1 teaspoon Worcestershire sauce

1 tablespoon chopped fresh flat-leaf parsley

10 ripe black olives, pitted and sliced

1 red bell pepper, seeded and chopped

6 ounces dried spaghetti

1⅔ cups freshly grated Parmesan cheese

salt and pepper

1. Preheat the oven to 400°F. Brush an 8-inch loose-bottom, round cake pan with oil and line the bottom with parchment paper. Heat half the oil in a skillet. Add the eggplants, in batches, and cook until lightly browned on both sides. Add more oil, as required. Drain the eggplants on paper towels, then arrange in overlapping slices to cover the bottom and sides of the cake pan, reserving a few slices.

2. Heat the remaining oil in a large saucepan and add the beef, onion, and garlic. Cook over medium heat, breaking up the meat with a wooden spoon, until browned all over. Add the tomato paste, tomatoes and their can juices, Worcestershire sauce, and parsley. Season with salt and pepper and simmer for 10 minutes. Add the olives and red bell pepper and cook for 10 minutes.

3. Meanwhile, bring a large saucepan of lightly salted water to a boil. Add the pasta, bring back to a boil, and cook for 8–10 minutes, or according to the package directions, until tender but still firm to the bite. Drain and transfer to a bowl. Add the meat sauce and cheese and toss, then spoon into the cake pan, press down, and cover with the remaining eggplant slices. Bake for 40 minutes. Let the cake stand for 5 minutes, then loosen around the edges and invert onto a plate. Remove and discard the parchment paper and serve immediately.

Beef & Pasta Bites

 SERVES 6

PREP TIME:
25 minutes

COOKING TIME:
1 hour

nutritional information per serving	800 cal, 44g fat, 19g sat fat, 7g total sugars, 1.1g salt

For a change of pace, try this delicious, deep-fried pasta treat—it will be a sure-fire hit with children.

INGREDIENTS

3 tablespoons olive oil

2 onions, chopped

2 garlic cloves, finely chopped

1 (14½-ounce) can diced tomatoes

1 teaspoon light brown sugar

½ cup water

12–16 dried cannelloni tubes

1 pound fresh ground beef

1 tablespoon chopped fresh flat-leaf parsley

pinch dried oregano

12 ounces mozzarella cheese, grated

1½ cups ricotta cheese

vegetable oil, for deep-frying

½ cups all-purpose flour

2 eggs, lightly beaten

1¾ cups fresh bread crumbs

salt and pepper

1. Heat 2 tablespoons of the olive oil in a saucepan, add half the chopped onions and garlic, and cook over low heat for 5 minutes. Stir in the tomatoes, sugar, and water and season with salt and pepper. Simmer, stirring occasionally, for 20 minutes. Remove from the heat, ladle ½ cup into a food processor or blender, and process to a coarse puree.

2. Bring a saucepan of lightly salted water to a boil. Add the pasta, bring back to a boil, and cook for 5–6 minutes. Drain and set aside on a dish towel.

3. Heat the remaining olive oil in a skillet, add the remaining onion and garlic, and cook over low heat, stirring occasionally, for 5 minutes. Increase the heat to medium, add the ground beef, and cook, stirring frequently, for 5–7 minutes, until brown. Reduce the heat, stir in the herbs and pureed tomato sauce, season with salt and pepper, and simmer for 10 minutes. Remove from the heat and let cool.

4. Stir the mozzarella cheese and ricotta cheese into the meat mixture, then use to fill the cannelloni tubes. Chill in the freezer for 5 minutes. Heat the vegetable oil to 350–375°F or until a cube of day-old bread browns in 30 seconds. Cut each cannelloni tube into three pieces. Coat them in the flour, then in the beaten egg, and, finally, in bread crumbs. Add to the hot oil, in batches, and cook for 4–5 minutes, until crisp and golden. Remove and drain on paper towels. Serve immediately.

Pork & Pasta Casserole

SERVES 4

PREP TIME:
15 minutes

COOKING TIME:
1½ hours

nutritional information per serving	860 cal, 46g fat, 23g sat fat, 11g total sugars, 1.6g salt

The flavor of olive oil is lost in cooking, so reserve more expensive extra virgin olive oil for other uses.

INGREDIENTS

2 tablespoons olive oil

1 onion, chopped

1 garlic clove, finely chopped

2 carrots, diced

2 ounces pancetta, chopped

1⅔ cups chopped button mushrooms

1 pound ground pork

½ cup dry white wine

¼ cup tomato puree

1 cup canned diced tomatoes

2 teaspoons chopped fresh sage or ½ teaspoon dried sage

8 ounces dried rigatoni

5 ounces mozzarella cheese, diced

¼ cup freshly grated Parmesan cheese

1¼ cups hot Classic White Sauce (see page 274)

salt and pepper

1. Preheat the oven to 400°F. Heat the olive oil in a large, heavy skillet. Add the onion, garlic, and carrots and cook over low heat, stirring occasionally, for 5 minutes, or until the onion has softened. Add the pancetta and cook for 5 minutes. Add the chopped mushrooms and cook, stirring occasionally, for an additional 2 minutes. Add the pork and cook, breaking it up with a wooden spoon, until the meat is browned all over. Stir in the wine, tomato puree, chopped tomatoes and their can juices, and sage. Season with salt and pepper and bring to a boil, then cover and simmer over low heat for 25–30 minutes.

2. Meanwhile, bring a large saucepan of lightly salted water to a boil. Add the pasta, bring back to a boil, and cook for 8–10 minutes, or according to the package directions, until tender but still firm to the bite.

3. Spoon the pork mixture into a large ovenproof dish. Stir the mozzarella cheese and half the Parmesan cheese into the Classic White Sauce. Drain the pasta and stir the sauce into it, then spoon it over the pork mixture. Sprinkle with the remaining Parmesan cheese and bake in the preheated oven for 25–30 minutes, until golden and bubbling. Serve immediately.

Ham & Pesto Lasagna

 SERVES 4–6   PREP TIME: 20 minutes   COOKING TIME: 1¼ hours

nutritional information per serving	545 cal, 29g fat, 13g sat fat, 7g total sugars, 2g salt

While still rich and satisfying, this is a lighter-tasting dish than the more usual lasagna made with ground beef.

INGREDIENTS

3 tablespoons butter

3 tablespoons all-purpose flour

1¼ cups whole milk

pinch of ground nutmeg

⅓ cup artichoke pesto or basil pesto

1 (12-ounce) package spinach, rinsed, drained, and trimmed

1 egg, lightly beaten

2 cups ricotta cheese

8 ounces cooked ham, diced

2 tomatoes, peeled, seeded, and diced

8 ounces dried oven-ready lasagna noodles

¼ cup freshly grated Parmesan cheese

salt and pepper

1. Preheat the oven to 400°F. Melt the butter in a saucepan, stir in the flour, and cook over low heat, stirring continuously, for 1 minute. Remove from the heat and gradually beat in the milk. Return to the heat and bring to a boil, beating continuously, until thickened and smooth. Remove from the heat and stir in the nutmeg and pesto.

2. Meanwhile, cook the spinach in just the water clinging to the leaves for 5–10 minutes, until wilted. Drain, squeeze out the excess moisture, and pat dry, then finely chop.

3. Stir the egg into the ricotta cheese and season with salt and pepper. Stir in the spinach, ham, and tomatoes.

4. Make alternating layers of lasagna, the cheese mixture, and the pesto sauce in an ovenproof dish, ending with a layer of lasagna topped with pesto sauce. Cover the dish with aluminum foil and bake in the preheated oven for 50 minutes.

5. Remove the dish from the oven, discard the foil, and sprinkle the top of the lasagna with the Parmesan cheese. Return to the oven and bake for an additional 5 minutes, until golden and bubbling. Let stand for 5 minutes before serving.

Chicken Ravioli in Tarragon Broth

SERVES 6

PREP TIME:
30–45 minutes
plus chilling

COOKING TIME:
1 hour

nutritional information per serving	267 cal, 8g fat, 4g sat fat, 0.6g total sugars, 1.4g salt

Ravioli are small squares of pasta stuffed with cheese, vegetables or meat. They are a classic Italian dish and usually served with a sauce or delicate broth.

INGREDIENTS

9 cups chicken stock

2 tablespoons finely chopped fresh tarragon leaves

freshly grated Parmesan cheese, to serve

pasta dough
1 cup all-purpose flour, plus extra if needed

2 tablespoons fresh tarragon leaves, stems removed

pinch of salt

1 egg

1 egg, separated

1 teaspoon extra virgin olive oil

2–3 tablespoons water

filling
1½ cups coarsely chopped, cooked chicken

½ teaspoon grated lemon rind

2 tablespoons chopped mixed fresh tarragon, chives, and parsley

¼ cup heavy whipping cream

salt and pepper

1. To make the pasta, combine the flour, tarragon, and salt in a food processor or blender. Beat together the egg, egg yolk, oil, and 2 tablespoons of water. With the machine running, pour in the egg mixture and process until it forms a ball. Wrap and chill in the refrigerator for 30 minutes. Reserve the egg white.

2. To make the filling, put the chicken, lemon rind, and mixed herbs in a food processor or blender and season with salt and pepper. Chop finely. Do not overprocess. Scrape into a bowl and stir in the cream.

3. Divide the pasta dough in half. Cover one half and roll out the other half on a floured surface to less than $\frac{1}{16}$ inch. Cut out rectangles measuring about 4 x 2 inches. Place a teaspoon of filling on one half of each rectangle. Brush the edges with egg white and fold in half. Press the edges to seal. Arrange on a baking sheet dusted with flour. Repeat with the remaining dough. Let the ravioli dry for about 15 minutes or chill for 1–2 hours in the refrigerator.

4. Bring a large saucepan of water to a boil. Drop in half of the ravioli and cook for 12–15 minutes, or until just tender. Drain on a dish towel while cooking the remainder.

5. Meanwhile, put the stock and tarragon in a large saucepan. Bring to a boil, then cover and simmer for 15 minutes. Add the ravioli and simmer for an additional 5 minutes. Ladle into warm bowls and serve immediately with Parmesan cheese.

Chicken & Mushroom Lasagna

 SERVES 4–6   PREP TIME: 15 minutes   COOKING TIME: 1½ hours

nutritional information per serving	534 cal, 25g fat, 11g sat fat, 9g total sugars, 1.1g salt

Lighter than a traditional lasagna, this is a great dish to serve when you have guests.

INGREDIENTS

2 tablespoons olive oil

1 large onion, finely chopped

1 pound fresh ground chicken or turkey

5 ounces smoked pancetta, chopped

4 cups chopped cremini mushrooms,

4 ounces dried porcini mushrooms, soaked

⅔ cup dry white wine

1 (14½-ounce) can diced tomatoes

3 tablespoons chopped fresh basil leaves

9 dried oven-ready lasagna noodles

3 tablespoons finely grated Parmesan cheese

salt and pepper

white sauce
2½ cups whole milk

4 tablespoons butter

½ cup all-purpose flour

1 bay leaf

1. Preheat the oven to 375°F. For the white sauce, heat the milk, butter, flour, and bay leaf in a saucepan, beating continuously, until smooth and thick. Season with salt and pepper, cover, and let stand.

2. Heat the oil in a large saucepan and sauté the onion, stirring, for 3–4 minutes. Add the chicken and pancetta and cook for 6–8 minutes. Stir in both types of mushrooms and cook for an additional 2–3 minutes.

3. Add the wine and bring to a boil. Pour in the tomatoes and their can juices, cover, and simmer for 20 minutes. Stir in the basil.

4. Arrange three of the lasagna noodles in a rectangular ovenproof dish, then spoon over one-third of the meat sauce. Remove and discard the bay leaf from the white sauce. Spread one-third of the sauce over the meat. Repeat the layers two times, finishing with a layer of white sauce.

5. Sprinkle with the cheese and bake in the preheated oven for 35–40 minutes, until the topping is golden and bubbling. Serve immediately.

Turkey & Mushroom Cannelloni

SERVES 4   PREP TIME: 15 minutes   COOKING TIME: 1¾ hours

nutritional information per serving | 925 cal, 48g fat, 26g sat fat, 15g total sugars, 2.6g salt

Cannelloni tubes filled with a delicious mix of mushrooms, chicken, and prosciutto make a wonderful main dish for a dinner party.

INGREDIENTS

butter, for greasing

2 tablespoons olive oil

2 garlic cloves, crushed

1 large onion, finely chopped

8 ounces wild mushrooms, sliced

12 ounces fresh ground turkey

4 ounces prosciutto, diced

⅔ cup Marsala

1 cup canned diced tomatoes

1 tablespoon shredded fresh basil leaves

2 tablespoons tomato paste

10–12 dried cannelloni tubes

2½ cups Classic White Sauce (see page 274)

1 cup freshly grated Parmesan cheese

salt and pepper

1. Preheat the oven to 375°F. Lightly grease a large ovenproof dish. Heat the oil in a heavy skillet. Add the garlic, onion, and mushrooms and cook over low heat, stirring frequently, for 8–10 minutes. Add the ground turkey and prosciutto and cook, stirring frequently, for 12 minutes, or until browned all over. Stir in the Marsala, tomatoes and their can juices, basil, and tomato paste and cook for 4 minutes. Season with salt and pepper, then cover and simmer for 30 minutes. Uncover, stir, and simmer for 15 minutes.

2. Meanwhile, bring a large saucepan of lightly salted water to a boil. Add the cannelloni tubes, bring back to a boil, and cook for 8–10 minutes, or according to the package directions, until tender but still firm to the bite. Using a slotted spoon, transfer the cannelloni tubes to a plate and pat dry with paper towels.

3. Using a teaspoon, fill the cannelloni tubes with the turkey-and-mushroom mixture. Transfer them to the dish. Pour the Classic White Sauce over them to cover completely and sprinkle with the grated Parmesan cheese.

4. Bake in the preheated oven for 30 minutes, or until golden and bubbling. Serve immediately.

Turkey Pasta Casserole

SERVES 4–6

PREP TIME:
15 minutes

COOKING TIME:
50 minutes

nutritional information per serving	614 cal, 27g fat, 15g sat fat, 8g total sugars, 1.1g salt

This fail-safe casserole is filling, easy to make, and economical—perfect for a midweek family dinner.

INGREDIENTS

1 stick butter

1 tablespoon olive oil

1 onion, finely chopped

1 pound fresh ground turkey

2 tablespoons all-purpose flour

3 cups whole milk

1 teaspoon Dijon mustard

¾ cup shredded cheddar cheese

10 ounces dried macaroni

2 tablespoons chopped fresh parsley

2 cups fresh bread crumbs

1. Melt 2 tablespoons of the butter with the oil in a skillet. Add the onion and cook over low heat, stirring occasionally, for 5 minutes, until soft. Add the turkey, increase the heat to medium, and cook, stirring frequently, for 7–8 minutes, until evenly browned. Remove the skillet from the heat, transfer the turkey and onion to a bowl with a slotted spoon, and set aside.

2. Melt 3 tablespoons of the remaining butter in a saucepan, stir in the flour, and cook, stirring continuously, for 1 minute. Remove the pan from the heat and gradually beat in the milk, then return to the heat and bring to a boil, beating continuously until thickened. Remove the pan from the heat and stir in the mustard, turkey mixture, and ½ cup of the cheese.

3. Preheat the oven to 350°F. Bring a large saucepan of lightly salted water to a boil. Add the pasta, bring back to a boil, and cook for 8–10 minutes, or according to the package directions, until tender but still firm to the bite. Drain and stir into the turkey mixture with the parsley.

4. Spoon the mixture into an ovenproof dish, sprinkle with the bread crumbs and remaining cheese, and dot with the remaining butter. Bake in the preheated oven for 25 minutes, until golden and bubbling. Serve immediately.

Pasticcio

SERVES 4

PREP TIME:
15 minutes

COOKING TIME:
1½ hours

nutritional information per serving	523 cal, 26g fat, 11g sat fat, 8g total sugars, 0.9g salt

This recipe shares its origins with a traditional Greek dish made with lamb. It is delicious served hot or cold.

INGREDIENTS

1 tablespoon olive oil
1 onion, chopped
2 garlic cloves, finely chopped
1 pound fresh ground lamb
2 tablespoons tomato paste
2 tablespoons all-purpose flour
1¼ cups chicken stock
1 teaspoon ground cinnamon
4 ounces dried macaroni
2 beefsteak tomatoes, sliced
1¼ cups Greek yogurt
2 eggs, lightly beaten
salt and pepper

1. Preheat the oven to 375°F. Heat the oil in a large, heavy skillet. Add the onion and garlic and cook over low heat, stirring occasionally, for 5 minutes, or until softened. Add the lamb and cook, breaking it up with a wooden spoon, until browned all over. Add the tomato paste and sprinkle in the flour. Cook, stirring, for 1 minute, then stir in the stock. Season with salt and pepper and stir in the cinnamon. Bring to a boil, reduce the heat, cover, and cook for 25 minutes.

2. Meanwhile, bring a large saucepan of lightly salted water to a boil. Add the pasta, bring back to a boil, and cook for 8–10 minutes, or according to the package directions, until tender but still firm to the bite.

3. Drain the pasta and stir into the lamb mixture. Spoon into a large ovenproof dish and arrange the tomato slices on top. Beat together the yogurt and eggs, then spoon the mixture evenly over the lamb. Bake in the preheated oven for 1 hour until golden and bubbling. Serve immediately.

1

3

3

VARIATION
Pasticcio doesn't have to be made with lamb. It is also delicious made with ground turkey or chicken.

Spinach & Tomato Tortellini Soup

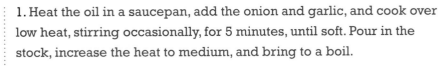

SERVES 4   PREP TIME: 10 minutes   COOKING TIME: 25 minutes

nutritional information per serving	512 cal, 22g fat, 6g sat fat, 11g total sugars, 1.7g salt

Serve this tasty soup with crusty bread for a filling meal-in-a-bowl lunch for the family.

INGREDIENTS

¼ cup olive oil

1 onion, thinly sliced

2 garlic cloves, finely chopped

3½ cups chicken stock

1 pound fresh or frozen chicken or pork tortellini

1 (14½-ounce) can diced tomatoes

1 tablespoon tomato paste

1 (15-ounce) can cranberry beans, drained

1 (12-ounce) package spinach, rinsed, drained, and trimmed

2 tablespoons chopped fresh flat-leaf parsley

salt and pepper

freshly grated Parmesan cheese, to serve

1. Heat the oil in a saucepan, add the onion and garlic, and cook over low heat, stirring occasionally, for 5 minutes, until soft. Pour in the stock, increase the heat to medium, and bring to a boil.

2. Add the tortellini and cook for 5 minutes, then reduce the heat, add the tomatoes and their can juices, tomato paste, and beans, and season with salt and pepper. Reduce the heat and simmer for an additional 5 minutes. Stir in the spinach and parsley and cook for 1–2 minutes, until the spinach is just wilted. Remove from the heat and serve immediately, with the cheese separately.

SOMETHING
DIFFERENT
For a vegetarian
version, substitute
tortellini stuffed
with ricotta cheese
or butternut
squash puree
and use vegetable
instead of
chicken stock.

Parmesan-Filled Tortellini Salad

 SERVES 4

PREP TIME:
15 minutes

COOKING TIME:
15–20 minutes
plus chilling

nutritional information per serving	591 cal, 42g fat, 8g sat fat, 13g total sugars, 2.6g salt

This salad works just as well as a side dish as it does as a main dish, and it's also perfect for picnics.

INGREDIENTS

½ cup olive oil

1 onion, thinly sliced

1 red bell pepper, seeded and thinly sliced

3 tablespoons balsamic vinegar

1 tablespoon chopped fresh thyme

1 pound tricolor Parmesan cheese tortellini

1 (14-ounce) can artichoke hearts, drained and sliced

8 cherry tomatoes, halved

1 cup ripe black olives, pitted and coarsely chopped

salt and pepper

1. Heat 2 tablespoons of the oil in a skillet, add the onion and red bell pepper, and cook over low heat, stirring occasionally, for 8–10 minutes, until the onion is just beginning to brown. Stir in the vinegar and thyme, season with salt, and remove the skillet from the heat.

2. Bring a large saucepan of lightly salted water to a boil. Add the pasta, bring back to a boil, and cook for 8–10 minutes, or according to the package directions, until tender but still firm to the bite. Drain well, transfer the pasta to a large bowl, add 2 tablespoons of the remaining oil and toss.

3. Add the artichoke hearts, tomatoes, and olives to the bowl. Add the pasta and the remaining oil, season with salt and pepper, and toss. Add the reserved onion and red pepper mixture and toss again. Cover with plastic wrap and chill in the refrigerator for at least two hours before serving.

This quantity
would serve
6-8 as a side
dish and would
be delicious
with broiled
chicken, steak,
or poached fish.

Spinach & Ricotta Cannelloni

 SERVES 4   PREP TIME: 20 minutes   COOKING TIME: 40–45 minutes

nutritional information per serving	591 cal, 28g fat, 16g sat fat, 9g total sugars, 1.1g salt

Cannelloni started life as sheets of pasta—lasagna noodles—which were rolled around a filling, but now tubes of pasta, ready for stuffing, are available.

INGREDIENTS

melted butter, for greasing

12 dried cannelloni tubes, each about 3 inches long

salt and pepper

filling
½ (10-ounce) package frozen spinach, thawed and drained

½ cup ricotta cheese

1 egg

3 tablespoons grated pecorino cheese

pinch of freshly grated nutmeg

cheese sauce
2 tablespoons butter

2 tablespoons all-purpose flour

2½ cups hot whole milk

¾ cup shredded Gruyère cheese

1. Preheat the oven to 350°F. Grease a rectangular ovenproof dish with the melted butter.

2. Bring a large saucepan of lightly salted water to a boil. Add the pasta, bring back to a boil, and cook for 6–7 minutes, or according to the package directions, until nearly tender. Drain and rinse, then spread out on a clean dish towel.

3. For the filling, put the spinach and ricotta into a food processor or blender and process briefly until combined. Add the egg and pecorino cheese and process to a smooth paste. Transfer to a bowl, add the nutmeg, and season with salt and pepper.

4. Spoon the filling into a pastry bag fitted with a ½-inch tip. Carefully open a cannelloni tube and pipe in a little of the filling. Place the filled tube in the prepared dish and repeat.

5. For the cheese sauce, melt the butter in a saucepan. Add the flour to the butter and cook over low heat, stirring continuously, for 1 minute. Remove from the heat and gradually stir in the hot milk. Return to the heat and bring to a boil, stirring continuously. Simmer over low heat, stirring frequently, for 10 minutes, until thickened and smooth.

6. Remove from the heat, stir in the Gruyère cheese, and season with salt and pepper.

7. Spoon the cheese sauce over the filled cannelloni. Cover the dish with aluminum foil and bake in the preheated oven for 20–25 minutes. Serve immediately.

Spicy Vegetable Lasagna

 SERVES 4

PREP TIME:
15 minutes
plus standing time

COOKING TIME:
55 minutes

nutritional information per serving	534 cal, 28g fat, 12g sat fat, 15g total sugars, 0.8g salt

This colorful and tasty lasagna has layers of diced and sliced vegetables in tomato sauce, all topped with a rich cheese sauce.

INGREDIENTS

1 eggplant, sliced
3 tablespoons olive oil
2 garlic cloves, crushed
1 red onion, halved and sliced
3 mixed bell peppers, seeded and diced
3 cups sliced button mushrooms,
2 celery stalks, sliced
1 zucchini, diced
½ teaspoon chili powder
½ teaspoon ground cumin
2 tomatoes, chopped
1¼ cups tomato paste
3 tablespoons chopped fresh basil
8 dried oven-ready lasagna noodles
salt and pepper

cheese sauce
2 tablespoons butter
1 tablespoon all-purpose flour
⅔ cup vegetable stock
1¼ cups whole milk
⅔ cup shredded cheddar cheese,
1 teaspoon Dijon mustard
1 egg, beaten

1. Place the eggplant slices in a colander, sprinkle with salt, and let stand for 20 minutes. Rinse under cold water, drain, and reserve.

2. Preheat the oven to 350°F. Heat the oil in a saucepan. Add the garlic and onion and sauté for 1–2 minutes. Add the bell peppers, mushrooms, celery, and zucchini and cook, stirring continuously, for 3–4 minutes.

3. Stir in the chili powder and cumin and cook for 1 minute. Mix in the tomatoes, tomato paste, and 2 tablespoons of the basil and season with salt and pepper.

4. For the sauce, melt the butter in a saucepan. Stir in the flour and cook for 1 minute. Remove from the heat, gradually stir in the stock and milk, return to the heat, then add half the cheese and all the mustard. Boil, stirring, until thickened. Stir in the remaining basil. Remove from the heat and stir in the egg.

5. Place half the lasagna noodles in an ovenproof dish. Top with half the vegetable and tomato sauce, then half the eggplants. Repeat and then spoon the cheese sauce on top. Sprinkle with the remaining cheese and bake in the preheated oven for 40 minutes, until golden and bubbling. Serve immediately.

Tuna Noodle Casserole

 SERVES 4

PREP TIME:
20 minutes

COOKING TIME:
35 minutes

nutritional information per serving	600 cal, 27g fat, 13g sat fat, 8g total sugars, 2.6g salt

Ever since canned condensed soups were invented in 1897, they have been used in casserole cooking. The most popular of these meals continues to be tuna noodle casserole.

INGREDIENTS

8 ounces dried tagliatelle

2 tablespoons butter

1¼ cups fresh bread crumbs

1 (14½-ounce) can condensed cream of mushroom soup

½ cup whole milk

2 celery stalks, chopped

1 red and 1 green bell pepper, seeded and chopped

1¼ cups shredded sharp cheddar cheese

2 tablespoons chopped fresh parsley

1 (5-ounce) can chunk light tuna in oil, drained and flaked

salt and pepper

1. Preheat the oven to 400°F. Bring a large saucepan of lightly salted water to a boil. Add the pasta and cook for 2 minutes less than the time specified in the package directions.

2. Meanwhile, melt the butter in a separate small saucepan over medium heat. Stir in the bread crumbs, then remove from the heat and reserve.

3. Drain the pasta thoroughly and reserve. Pour the soup into the pasta pan over medium heat, then stir in the milk, celery, bell peppers, half the cheese, and all the parsley. Add the tuna and gently stir in so that the flakes don't break up. Season with salt and pepper. Heat just until small bubbles appear around the edge of the mixture—do not boil.

4. Stir the pasta into the pan and use two forks to mix together all the ingredients. Spoon the mixture into an ovenproof dish and spread out. Stir the remaining cheese into the buttered bread crumbs, then sprinkle over the top of the pasta mixture. Bake in the preheated oven for 20–25 minutes, until golden and bubbling. Let stand for 5 minutes before serving.

Salmon Lasagna Rolls

 SERVES 4   PREP TIME: 15 minutes   COOKING TIME: 1 hour

nutritional information per serving	487 cal, 22g fat, 9g sat fat, 9g total sugars, 0.6g salt

This attractive and colorful dish is much easier to make than you might think and is well worth a little extra time.

INGREDIENTS

vegetable oil, for brushing

8 dried lasagna verde noodles

2 tablespoons butter

1 onion, sliced

½ red bell pepper, seeded and chopped

1 zucchini, diced

1 teaspoon chopped fresh ginger

4 ounces oyster mushrooms, torn into pieces

8 ounces salmon fillet, skinned and cut into chunks

3 tablespoons dry sherry

2 teaspoons cornstarch

3 tablespoons all-purpose flour

1¾ cups whole milk

¼ cup shredded cheddar cheese

1 tablespoon fresh white bread crumbs

salt and pepper

1. Preheat the oven to 400°F. Brush an ovenproof dish with oil. Bring a large saucepan of lightly salted water to a boil. Add the pasta, bring back to a boil, and cook for 8–10 minutes, or according to the package directions, until tender but still firm to the bite. Remove with tongs and drain on a clean dish towel.

2. Meanwhile, melt half the butter in a saucepan. Add the onion and cook over low heat, stirring occasionally, for 5 minutes, until softened. Add the red bell pepper, zucchini, and ginger and cook, stirring occasionally, for 10 minutes. Add the mushrooms and salmon and cook for 2 minutes, then mix together the sherry and cornstarch and stir into the pan. Cook for an additional 4 minutes, until the fish is opaque and flakes easily. Season with salt and pepper and remove the pan from the heat.

3. Melt the remaining butter in another pan. Stir in the flour and cook, stirring continuously, for 2 minutes. Gradually stir in the milk, then cook, stirring continuously, for 10 minutes. Remove the pan from the heat, stir in half the cheddar cheese and season with salt and pepper.

4. Spoon the salmon filling along one of the shorter sides of each lasagna noodle. Roll up and place in the prepared dish. Pour the sauce over the rolls and sprinkle with the bread crumbs and remaining cheese. Bake in the preheated oven for 15–20 minutes, until golden and bubbling. Serve immediately.

Macaroni & Seafood Casserole

 SERVES 4   PREP TIME: 10 minutes   COOKING TIME: 50 minutes

nutritional information per serving	825 cal, 42g fat, 21g sat fat, 12g total sugars, 2.7g salt

Fennel imparts a delicate anise flavor to dishes and goes particularly well with fish.

INGREDIENTS

12 ounces dried macaroni

3 ounces butter, plus extra for greasing

2 small fennel bulbs, trimmed and thinly sliced

6 ounces mushrooms, thinly sliced

6 ounces cooked peeled shrimp

pinch of cayenne pepper

2½ cups Classic White Sauce

2 ounces freshly grated Parmesan cheese

2 large tomatoes, halved and sliced

olive oil, for brushing

1 teaspoon dried oregano

salt

1. Preheat the oven to 350°F. Bring a large saucepan of lightly salted water to a boil. Add the pasta, bring back to a boil and cook for 8–10 minutes, or according to the package directions, until tender but still firm to the bite.

2. Drain and return to the saucepan. Add 25 g/1 ounce of the butter to the pasta, cover, shake the saucepan and keep warm.

3. Melt the remaining butter in a separate saucepan. Add the fennel and cook for 3–4 minutes. Stir in the mushrooms and cook for an additional 2 minutes. Stir in the shrimp, then remove the pan from the heat. Stir the cooked pasta, cayenne pepper and shrimp mixture into the Classic White Sauce.

4. Grease a large ovenproof dish, then pour the mixture into the dish and spread evenly. Sprinkle over the Parmesan cheese and arrange the tomato slices in a ring around the edge. Brush the tomatoes with oil, then sprinkle over the oregano. Bake in the preheated oven for 25 minutes, until golden and bubbling. Serve immediately.

Simple Butter Sauce

SERVES 4

PREP TIME:
15 minutes

COOKING TIME:
15 minutes

nutritional information
per serving

562 cal, 26g fat, 15g sat fat, 2g total sugars, 0.5g salt

*Delicious and made in minutes, this is a great
way to serve any long pasta, such as linguine,
for a midweek family meal.*

INGREDIENTS

1 pound dried long pasta

1 stick butter

8 sage leaves, finely chopped

8 basil leaves, finely chopped

½ bunch fresh flat-leaf parsley,
finely chopped

6 fresh thyme sprigs,
finely chopped

1 small bunch of chives, snipped

salt and pepper

freshly grated Parmesan cheese,
to serve

1. Bring a large saucepan of lightly salted water to a boil. Add the pasta, bring back to a boil, and cook for 8–10 minutes, or according to the package directions, until tender but still firm to the bite.

2. Just before the pasta is ready, melt the butter in a saucepan over low heat. Drain the pasta and pour the melted butter into the pan with the pasta. Add all the herbs, season with salt and pepper, and toss until the pasta strands are coated and glistening.

3. Divide among warm plates and serve immediately, with the Parmesan cheese served separately.

SOMETHING
DIFFERENT
Vary the herbs to
suit your personal
taste, but be careful
with pungent herbs,
such as tarragon
and marjoram.

Basic Tomato Sauce

 SERVES 4   PREP TIME: 15 minutes   COOKING TIME: 25–30 minutes

nutritional information per serving	124 cal, 11g fat, 4g sat fat, 5g total sugars, 0.2g salt

There is no question that this is Italy's most favorite sauce for serving with pasta as well as other ingredients.

INGREDIENTS

2 tablespoons butter

2 tablespoons olive oil

1 onion, finely chopped

1 garlic clove, finely chopped

1 celery stalk, finely chopped

1 (14½-ounce) can diced tomatoes or 8 plum tomatoes, peeled, cored, and chopped

2 tablespoons tomato paste

brown sugar, to taste

1 tablespoon chopped fresh herbs and/or 1–2 teaspoons dried herbs and/ or 1–2 bay leaves

½ cup water

salt and pepper

1. Melt the butter with the oil in a saucepan. Add the onion, garlic, and celery and cook over low heat, stirring occasionally, for 5 minutes, until softened.

2. Stir in the tomatoes, tomato paste, sugar to taste, the herbs, and water, and season with salt and pepper.

3. Increase the heat to medium and bring to a boil, then reduce the heat and simmer, stirring occasionally, for 15–20 minutes, until thickened. Use as required.

GOES WELL WITH

This all-purpose sauce may be served with almost any kind of pasta, especially ridged and curly types, and is also delicious baked with ravioli.

Parsley & Almond Pesto

SERVES 4   PREP TIME: 15 minutes   COOKING TIME: no cooking

nutritional information per serving	282 cal, 28g fat, 5g sat fat, 0.6g total sugars, 0.2g salt

As well as being a slightly sweet and refreshing sauce to serve with pasta, this quick sauce is great with poached fish.

INGREDIENTS

1 cup flat-leaf parsley, coarse stems removed
2 garlic cloves, coarsely chopped
3 tablespoons blanched almonds
½ cup olive oil
½ cup grated pecorino cheese
salt and pepper

1. Put the parsley, garlic, and almonds in a food processor or blender, season with salt and pepper, and process until minced.

2. With the motor running on slow speed, gradually add the oil in a slow, steady stream, until a smooth paste forms. Add the cheese and pulse a few times to combine.

3. Taste and adjust the seasoning, if necessary, and heat gently—do not boil. Use as required.

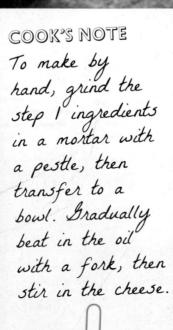

COOK'S NOTE
To make by hand, grind the step 1 ingredients in a mortar with a pestle, then transfer to a bowl. Gradually beat in the oil with a fork, then stir in the cheese.

Spicy Alfredo Sauce

 SERVES 4   PREP TIME: 10 minutes   COOKING TIME: 10 minutes

nutritional information per serving	799 cal, 44g fat, 27g sat fat, 3g total sugars, 0.5g salt

Alfredo di Lelio invented his classic cream, butter, and Parmesan sauce in Rome in 1914 and since then it has been modified in dozens of ways.

INGREDIENTS

1 pound dried fettuccine or other pasta

4 tablespoons butter

1–2 chiles, finely chopped

1 cup heavy cream

⅔ cup freshly grated Parmesan cheese

salt and pepper

1. Bring a large saucepan of lightly salted water to a boil. Add the pasta, bring back to a boil, and cook for 8–10 minutes, or according to the package directions, until tender but still firm to the bite.

2. Meanwhile, melt half the butter in another saucepan, add the chiles, and cook over low heat, stirring occasionally, for 3 minutes. Pour in ⅔ cup of the cream, increase the heat to medium, and bring to a boil. Reduce the heat and simmer for 1–2 minutes, until slightly thickened. Remove the pan from the heat.

3. Drain the pasta and transfer to the pan with the cream sauce. Return to the heat and lightly toss, then add the cheese and the remaining butter and cream. Season with salt and pepper and toss for 2–3 minutes, until the pasta is thoroughly coated in the sauce. Remove from the heat and serve immediately.

SOMETHING DIFFERENT
For a more substantial dish, add some strips of prosciutto or shredded cooked chicken in step 3.

Arrabiata Sauce

 SERVES 4   PREP TIME: 15 minutes   COOKING TIME: 30 minutes

nutritional information per serving	518 cal, 16g fat, 2.5g sat fat, 6g total sugars, trace salt

Serve this tangy hot tomato sauce with pasta shapes, such as penne, or spaghetti. Unlike many other tomato sauce and pasta dishes, it is not traditionally served with grated Parmesan cheese.

INGREDIENTS

⅔ cup dry white wine

1 tablespoon tomato paste

2 fresh red chiles, seeded and chopped

2 garlic cloves, finely chopped

¼ cup chopped fresh flat-leaf parsley

salt and pepper

3 ounces pecorino cheese shavings

sugocasa

⅓ cup extra virgin olive oil

8 plum tomatoes, chopped

salt and pepper

1. To make the sugocasa, heat the oil in a frying pan over a high heat until almost smoking. Add the tomatoes and cook, stirring frequently, for 2–3 minutes.

2. Reduce the heat to low and cook gently for 20 minutes, or until very soft. Season with salt and pepper. Press through a nonmetallic strainer into a saucepan.

3. Add the wine, tomato paste, chiles, and garlic to the sugocasa, and bring to a boil. Reduce the heat and simmer gently. Check and adjust the seasoning, then stir in the parsley and the cheese. Use as require.

Chipotle Pasta Sauce

 SERVES 4

PREP TIME:
45 minutes

COOKING TIME:
15 minutes

nutritional information per serving	166 cal, 16g fat, 1g sat fat, 3g total sugars, trace salt

Smoking jalapeño chiles to make chipotles gives them a delicious depth of flavor but they do remain fiery.

INGREDIENTS

2 ancho chiles, seeded

1 red bell pepper

1–2 canned jalepeno or chipotle chiles, drained

⅓ cup pine nuts

juice of ½ lime

2 garlic cloves, coarsely chopped

1 tablespoon olive oil

salt

1. Preheat the broiler. Meanwhile put the ancho chiles into a bowl, pour in enough hot water to cover, and let soak for 30 minutes.

2. Put the red bell pepper on a baking sheet and place under the broiler, turning occasionally, for about 15 minutes, until charred and blistered. Remove with tongs, put into a plastic food bag, tie the top, and let cool.

3. Drain the ancho chiles, reserving 1 tablespoon of the soaking liquid. Peel, seed, and coarsely chop the red bell pepper.

4. Put the ancho chiles, reserved soaking liquid, red bell pepper, chipotle chiles, pine nuts, 1 tablespoon of the lime juice, and the garlic into a food processor or blender and process to a smooth paste. With the motor running at low speed, add the oil and process until thoroughly combined. If the sauce is too thick, add a little more lime juice and process briefly again. Season with salt and use as required.

FREEZING TIP

Freeze the sauce in an airtight container for 1-2 weeks.

Creole Sauce

 SERVES 4   PREP TIME:
15 minutes   COOKING TIME:
35–40 minutes

nutritional information per serving	127 cal, 6.5g fat, 1g sat fat, 10g total sugars, 0.2g salt

Enjoy a taste of the Deep South with this vibrant, spicy sauce, the chopped okra lending it both characteristic flavor and thickness.

INGREDIENTS

2 tablespoons sunflower oil

1 red bell pepper, seeded and thinly sliced

1 green bell pepper, seeded and thinly sliced

1 onion, thinly sliced

2–3 garlic cloves, crushed

1 fresh red chile, seeded and chopped

1 teaspoon ground coriander

1 teaspoon ground cumin

4 ripe tomatoes, peeled and chopped

1¼ cups vegetable stock

10 okra pods, trimmed and chopped

1 tablespoon chopped fresh cilantro

salt and pepper

1. Heat the oil in a heavy saucepan, add the red bell pepper, green bell pepper, onion, garlic, and chile and sauté, stirring frequently, for 3 minutes. Add the ground coriander and cumin and sauté, stirring frequently, for an additional 3 minutes.

2. Stir in the tomatoes and stock and bring to a boil. Reduce the heat and simmer, stirring occasionally, for 15 minutes, or until the sauce has reduced slightly.

3. Add the okra to the pan with salt and pepper and simmer for an additional 10–15 minutes, or until the sauce has thickened. Stir in the fresh cilantro and use as required.

Four Cheese Sauce

 SERVES 4   PREP TIME: 15 minutes   COOKING TIME: 8–10 minutes

nutritional information per serving	879 cal, 44g fat, 27g sat fat, 2.5g total sugars, 2.5g salt

This sauce is actually made in the serving dish containing the drained pasta, and it must be one of the quickest sauces to prepare!

INGREDIENTS

1 pound dried tagliatelle

4 tablespoons butter

⅔ cup crumbled Gorgonzola cheese or other blue cheese

3 ounces fontina cheese, cut into narrow julienne strips

3 ounces Gruyère cheese, cut into julienne strips

3 ounces Parmesan cheese, cut into julienne strips

salt

1. Bring a large saucepan of lightly salted water to a boil. Add the pasta, bring back to a boil, and cook for 8–10 minutes, or according to the package directions, until tender but still firm to the bite.

2. Meanwhile, put the butter in a heatproof bowl set over a saucepan of barely simmering water. When it has melted, continue to heat it until hot but not boiling.

3. Drain the pasta and transfer to a warm serving bowl. Spread the cheeses on top and pour the hot butter over the cheeses and pasta. Toss lightly and serve immediately.

1   2   3

SOMETHING
DIFFERENT
You can substitute
strips of provolone for
the Gorgonzola for a
more subtle flavor.

Mushroom Sauce

 SERVES 4

PREP TIME:
10 minutes

COOKING TIME:
20 minutes

nutritional information per serving	746 cal, 43g fat, 20g sat fat, 5g total sugars, 0.3g salt

This is a delicious pasta sauce, which uses sun-dried tomatoes and cremini mushrooms. It's made even more luxurious with the addition of heavy cream and port.

INGREDIENTS

4 tablespoons butter

1 tablespoon olive oil

6 shallots, sliced

1 pound cremini mushrooms, sliced

1 teaspoon all-purpose flour

⅔ cup heavy cream

2 tablespoons port

¾ cup drained and chopped sun-dried tomatoes in oil

pinch of freshly grated nutmeg

salt and pepper

2 tablespoons chopped fresh flat-leaf parsley, to garnish

1. Melt the butter with the oil in a large, heavy skillet. Add the shallots and cook over low heat, stirring occasionally, for 4–5 minutes, or until softened. Add the mushrooms and cook over low heat for an additional 2 minutes. Season with salt and pepper, sprinkle in the flour and cook, stirring, for 1 minute.

2. Remove the skillet from the heat and gradually stir in the cream and port. Return to the heat, add the sun-dried tomatoes and grated nutmeg, and cook over low heat, stirring occasionally, for 8 minutes. Use as required.

1

1

2

TO SERVE

Nutmeg is used widely in Italian cooking because it has a fragrant, sweet aroma. Use freshly grated nutmeg instead of ground, which deteriorates rapidly. Store it in an airtight container.

Tomato, Mushroom & Bacon Sauce

 SERVES 2   PREP TIME: 20 minutes   COOKING TIME: 30–35 minutes

nutritional information per serving	231 cal, 17g fat, 6g sat fat, 9g total sugars, 1.8g salt

In this dish, fresh tomatoes make a delicious Italian-style sauce, which goes particularly well with pasta.

INGREDIENTS

1 tablespoon olive oil

1 small onion, finely chopped

1–2 garlic cloves, crushed

3 tomatoes, peeled and chopped

2 teaspoons tomato paste

2 tablespoons water

4 ounces lean bacon, diced

½ cup sliced button mushrooms

1 tablespoon chopped fresh parsley or 1 teaspoon chopped fresh cilantro

2 tablespoons sour cream (optional)

salt and pepper

freshly cooked pasta, to serve

1. Heat the oil in a saucepan over low heat, add the onion and garlic, and sauté gently.

2. Add the tomatoes, tomato paste, and water to the mixture in the pan, season with salt and pepper, and bring to a boil. Cover and simmer gently for 10 minutes.

3. Heat the bacon gently in a skillet until the fat runs, add the mushrooms, and continue cooking for 3–4 minutes. Drain off any excess fat.

4. Add the bacon and mushrooms to the tomato mixture, together with the parsley and the sour cream, if using. Reheat the sauce gently, then pour over the pasta and toss well. Serve immediately.

Pumpkin Sauce

SERVES 4

PREP TIME: 15 minutes

COOKING TIME: 1¼ hours

nutritional information per serving	295 cal, 28g fat, 16g sat fat, 6g total sugars, 0.6g salt

This subtle and unusual sauce has a velvety texture, looks fabulous, and tastes simply superb.

INGREDIENTS

4 tablespoons butter

6 shallots, minced

7 cups pumpkin, acorn squash, or butternut squash cubes

pinch of freshly grated nutmeg

1 cup light cream

¼ cup freshly grated Parmesan cheese, plus extra to serve

2 tablespoons chopped fresh flat-leaf parsley

salt

1. Melt the butter in a large, heavy saucepan. Add the shallots, sprinkle with a little salt, cover, and cook over low heat, stirring occasionally, for 30 minutes.

2. Add the pumpkin pieces and season with nutmeg. Cover and cook over low heat, stirring occasionally, for 40 minutes, or until the pumpkin is pulpy. Stir in the cream, cheese, and parsley and remove the pan from the heat.

3. Stir the pumpkin mixture and add a little water if the mixture seems too thick. Use as required.

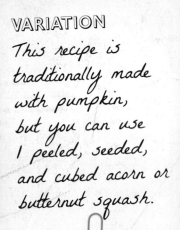

VARIATION
This recipe is
traditionally made
with pumpkin,
but you can use
1 peeled, seeded,
and cubed acorn or
butternut squash.

Garlic Walnut Sauce

 SERVES 4

PREP TIME:
15 minutes

COOKING TIME:
15–20 minutes

nutritional information
per serving

311 cal, 29g fat, 12g sat fat, 3g total sugars, 0.5g salt

*This rich pasta sauce is for garlic lovers everywhere.
It is quick and easy to prepare and full of flavor.*

INGREDIENTS

2 tablespoons walnut oil

1 bunch of scallions, sliced

2 garlic cloves, thinly sliced

3 cups sliced button mushrooms,

1 (10-ounce) pacakge frozen
spinach, thawed and drained

½ cup cream cheese with
garlic and herbs

¼ cup light cream

½ cup unsalted pistachio nuts,
chopped

1. Heat the walnut oil in a large skillet. Add the scallions and garlic and sauté for 1 minute, or until just softened. Add the mushrooms, stir well, cover, and cook over low heat for 5 minutes, or until just softened but not browned.

2. Add the spinach to the skillet and cook for 1–2 minutes. Add the cheese and heat until slightly melted. Stir in the cream and pistachio nuts and cook gently, without letting the mixture boil, until warm. Use as required.

GOES WELL WITH
This is especially delicious with pasta filled with cheese and herbs or other greens and is also tasty simply served with ribbon pasta.

Red Wine Sauce

 SERVES 4

 PREP TIME:
15 minutes

COOKING TIME:
20 minutes

nutritional information per serving	240 cal, 20g fat, 10g sat fat, 2.5g total sugars, 0.6g salt

Mushrooms are more usually cooked with white wine, but the robust earthy flavor of wild mushrooms is perfectly complemented with red wine in this sauce.

INGREDIENTS

½–1 stick butter

12 ounces mixed wild mushrooms, halved or quartered, if large

2 garlic cloves, finely chopped

1 tablespoon olive oil

¼ cup tomato paste

1 cup full-bodied red wine

½ cup pitted and halved ripe black olives

1 tablespoon chopped fresh parsley

salt and pepper

1. Melt 2 tablespoons of the butter in a skillet, add the mushrooms, sprinkle with a little salt, and cook over high heat, stirring occasionally, for 5 minutes.

2. Reduce the heat under the skillet to low, stir in the garlic and oil, and cook for 2 minutes, then stir in the tomato paste and cook for an additional 2 minutes.

3. Pour in the wine and cook for about 5 minutes, until the alcohol has evaporated. Meanwhile, dice the remaining butter. Add the butter to the skillet, one pat at a time, gently swirling the skillet until the butter has melted. Stir in the olives, season with salt and pepper, and remove the skillet from the heat. Sprinkle with parsley and use as required.

White Wine Sauce

 SERVES 4

PREP TIME:
15 minutes

COOKING TIME:
25 minutes

nutritional information per serving	844 cal, 77g fat, 48g sat fat, 4.5g total sugars, 1.2g salt

This rich, creamy sauce goes well with filled pasta such as ravioli—use a stock that matches the filling for extra flavor.

INGREDIENTS

1 Bermuda onion, chopped

5 cups dry white wine

10½ cups vegetable, chicken or fish stock

5 cups heavy cream

3 sticks butter

bunch of fresh flat-leaf parsley, finely chopped

salt and pepper

1. Put the onion in a large saucepan, pour in the wine, bring to a boil, and cook over high heat for 10 minutes, until the wine has almost completely evaporated.

2. Pour in the stock, return to a boil, and cook for 10-15 minutes, until it has reduced by two-thirds.

3. Stir in the cream and cook for 5 minutes, then stir in the butter, a little at a time. Add the parsley, season to taste with salt and pepper, and use as required.

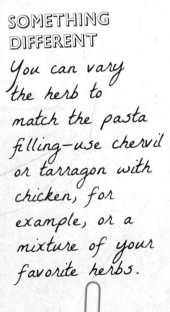

SOMETHING
DIFFERENT
You can vary
the herb to
match the pasta
filling—use chervil
or tarragon with
chicken, for
example, or a
mixture of your
favorite herbs.

Vodka Sauce

nutritional information per serving	582 cal, 52g fat, 32g sat fat, 8g total sugars, 0.5g salt

This exotic creamy sauce has become popular in trendy restaurants in the last few years, but is surprisingly easy to make.

INGREDIENTS

4 tablespoons butter
1 onion, finely chopped
½ cup vodka
1 (28-ounce) can diced tomatoes
1¼ cups heavy cream
salt and pepper

1. Melt the butter in a large saucepan, add the onion, and cook over low heat, stirring occasionally, for 8–10 minutes, until just beginning to brown.

2. Add the vodka and simmer for 10 minutes, then stir in the tomatoes, crushing them gently with a wooden spoon. Simmer, stirring occasionally, for 25 minutes.

3. Stir in the cream, season with salt and pepper, and simmer for an additional 30 minutes. Do not let the sauce boil. Remove from the heat and use as required.

SOMETHING DIFFERENT
To add a spicy kick, stir ½ teaspoon of crushed red pepper into the vodka and let steep for 10 minutes before straining the vodka into the pan.

Spicy Crab Sauce

SERVES 4

PREP TIME: 15–20 minutes

COOKING TIME: 5-10 minutes

nutritional information per serving	336 cal, 22g fat, 3g sat fat, 0.3g total sugars, 0.9g salt

This sauce is probably one of the simplest in the book, yet the result is as impressive as a sauce that takes a long time to prepare.

INGREDIENTS

1 dressed crab, about 1 pound (including the shell)

⅓ cup extra-virgin olive oil

1 fresh red chile, seeded and finely chopped

2 garlic cloves, finely chopped

3 tablespoons chopped fresh parsley

2 tablespoons lemon juice

1 teaspoon finely grated lemon zest

salt and pepper

1. Scoop the meat from the crab shell into a bowl. Lightly mix together the white and brown meat and set aside.

2. Heat 2 tablespoons of the olive oil in a skillet. Add the chile and garlic. Cook for 30 seconds, then add the crabmeat, parsley, lemon juice, and lemon zest. Sauté over low heat for an additional 1 minute, or until the crab meat is just heated through.

3. Add the remaining olive oil to the sauce and season with salt and pepper. Use as required.

2　　2　　2

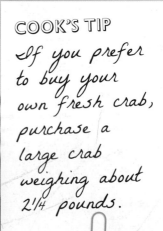

Seafood Sauce

 SERVES 4   PREP TIME: 15 minutes   COOKING TIME: 25–30 minutes

nutritional information per serving	232 cal, 10g fat, 2g sat fat, 0.2g total sugars, 0.9g salt

This is a great pasta sauce for informal entertaining because it is so quick and easy to make.

INGREDIENTS

1½ pounds fresh clams, or 1 (10-ounce) can clams, drained

2 tablespoons olive oil

2 garlic cloves, finely chopped

1 (14-ounce) package mixed prepared seafood, such as shrimp, squid, and mussels, defrosted if frozen

⅔ cup white wine

⅔ cup fish stock

2 tablespoons chopped fresh tarragon

salt and pepper

1. If using fresh clams, scrub them clean and discard any that are already open.

2. Heat the oil in a large skillet. Add the garlic and clams and cook for 2 minutes, shaking the skillet to make sure that all of the clams are coated in the oil. Add the remaining seafood to the skillet and cook for an additional 2 minutes.

3. Pour the wine and stock over the mixed seafood and garlic and bring to a boil. Cover the skillet, then lower the heat and simmer for 8–10 minutes, or until the shells open. Discard any clams that do not open.

4. Stir the tarragon into the sauce and season with salt and pepper. Use as required.